AND THEN CAME CAME THE ANGELS

BETH GAYLE

Whitman
Publishing, LLC
PUBLISHING SINCE 1934
www.whitman.com

www.whitman.com

3101 Clairmont Road • Suite G • Atlanta GA 30329

And Then Came the Angels
© 2012 Beth Gayle

Correspondence concerning this book may be directed to the publisher at the address above, Attn: And Then Came the Angels.

ISBN: 0794837433
Printed in the United States of America

DEDICATION

This dedication is from our family, as a whole.
God, of course, is our first and highest dedication;
always has been, always will be.

We also dedicate this book to our earthly angels. Some are family, some are friends, and some are strangers who have become family and friends. All in their own way have given of their time, talent, or treasure to help make us whole again.

Angels, we will never be able to thank you in a way that equals what you've done for us. We can only hope that when you read this book of our journey—a journey you helped carry us through—you will feel the depth of our gratitude. It's impossible to list you all by name, but oh how we wish we could. Please know that your names and your kindnesses are forever engraved in our hearts.

Dr. Donald Leslie, medical director of Shepherd Center in Atlanta, Georgia, is one of the angels who became like family to us. His dedication reaches well beyond his medical practice. He has spent a lifetime helping others, and his commitment to serve is evident in every aspect of his life. We simply wouldn't be here today if not for his heartfelt devotion to medicine *and* to our family. We are richly blessed to know and love him.

Beyond that, we want to thank Dr. Leslie and Harold Anderson for their kindness in helping this story find its way from our hearts to publication.

And last, but certainly not least, we dedicate this book to Chuck Scott. Chuck was our son's high school football coach. He was also the leader and mentor of his high school Christian youth group, Young Life. Over the years, they became great friends.

As you read this book, you will see that Chuck has an amazing heart. The way he spread his wings over our family is indescribable. No matter what our needs were, Chuck found a way to meet them. He dedicated several years of his life to bringing hope, help, and humor into our lives at a time when we could barely breathe. How do you thank someone for that?

A wise man once said,
"The best way to find yourself is to lose yourself in service to others."
Wow, did he know of our angels! He certainly knew of their hearts.

To all of our earthly angels:
May God bless you and your families
as you have so lovingly and abundantly blessed ours.

Forever grateful,
Richard, Beth, Gip, and Taylor

CONTENTS

Preface

And So the Story Goes

"Mr. Gayle, this is the Vidalia sheriff.
Your son's been shot in a hunting accident.
You need to get here immediately!"

L ife can be very unpredictable. Sometimes our days are running smoothly, and we seem to glide, almost effortlessly, through them. But other times life can take an unexpected turn, and suddenly our days aren't running *smoothly* at all. When a crisis comes along, it can catch us totally off-guard, and we may find ourselves engulfed in heartaches, fear, and uncertainty. How do we handle that?

Well, over the past few years, I've felt a pressing on my heart to write about our family's journey of "handling that." At first I was confused by this prompting, as I am not a professional writer or theologian. Yes, I have quite a miraculous story to tell. But I wasn't sure if I could write about it, let alone carry a message through it. So I thought I misunderstood God's pressing, and I dismissed it. But *He* didn't. *He kept pressing!* It seems He wants me to share not only what we've been through but also, and more importantly, *how* we got through it.

I honestly don't know how these pages will get from me to you. But just as God has led me to write, so shall He lead others to read . . . all in His divine timing.

Already I feel a lump in my throat knowing that in order to share our passage, I'll have to revisit some painful memories—memories I'd comfortably buried years ago. But to whom much is given, much is expected. And although we have not been spared heartache or devastation, we *have* been divinely nurtured through it. That is what this story is all about. Somehow we've found hope, healing, and even humor in places it didn't seem to exist. Much has been given.

So sit down, buckle up, and hold on tight because I'm about to take you on quite a ride. As I share our journey, I will tell you about the remarkable goodness we've seen in all this, as God has left His fingerprint on every page of our story. But I will also recount the depths of our despair. For you simply cannot grasp the magnitude of this miracle if you do not know of the fires from which God helped us emerge.

As I prepare to write, I pray I can do justice in describing His gracious love, His mighty strength, and His heavenly angels . . . right here on earth.

And so the story goes: on September 6, 2003, our lives were shattered.

And then came the angels!

Gip Growing Up

Gip's first birthday party was held in May 1985. Since Gip was the first grandchild on my side of the family, this was quite a family celebration! My parents (Honey and Pops) and Richard's parents (Mimi and Poppi) gathered in Louisiana, along with many of Richard's and my siblings. The party featured a birthday cake bigger than Gip himself!

From the time he was a toddler, Gip was already being groomed to be an LSU fan by the entire family. In fact, Mimi and Poppi bought him his first LSU football uniform and helmet. He slept in it for weeks. Who knew that, even growing up in Atlanta, his loyalty to LSU would endure? Both Richard and I grew up in Baton Rouge and went to LSU, so Gip's being a Tiger fan was inevitable.

Even as a little boy, Gip was aware that faith and prayer were important to our entire family. Here he prays with Pops before bedtime, as he always did during family visits to Honey and Pops. It was the family tradition to start a prayer by thanking God for all the blessings of the day, and to finish by praying for God's blessing on others.

Gip meets his new little brother, Taylor, for the first time. One of Gip's first questions about Taylor was "Dad, can he play ball?" Sure enough, in years to come, Gip and Taylor would carry on the family tradition of athletics. Sports was their whole world!

This family photo was taken on the occasion of Taylor's first Easter, once again celebrated with family in Louisiana. As you can see, Gip is beaming with pride over his baby brother—in fact, in church that day he introduced Taylor to every person in the pew!

In another classic big-brother moment, Gip gives Taylor his bottle.

It doesn't often snow in Atlanta enough to build a snowman, so this was a rare treat. Gip and Taylor gathered snow from almost every yard in our neighborhood, and as always, our family dog Yeller was at their side. Yeller was a gift from a friend, and a case of love at first sight for all three of them.

The photographer was a bit surprised that Gip and Taylor wanted to include Yeller in their studio portrait, but he allowed her to come in anyway and join them in their photo. He could tell that the three of them were inseparable.

Richard, Taylor, Gip, and friends in one of their many muscle-man competitions!

Gip shows off his first big purchase to Taylor: his first car, bought with his earnings from years of working for a landscaping company. Gip named "her" Big Dog.

Gip playing baseball at Collins Hill High School in Suwanee, Georgia. Sports are a big part of our family tradition, and Gip was following in his dad's footsteps in many ways. Richard played football and baseball all through school, and his father, Poppi, was a semi-professional baseball player. Richard enjoyed coaching both Gip and Taylor in baseball and football throughout their years in Little League.

As a boy, Gip had dreamed of playing high school baseball, and in his freshman year at CHHS he was selected as the first-string shortstop. This was quite a thrill, given that he was one of only 18 kids chosen to be on the team out of the nearly 200 who tried out.

Gip was also fortunate enough to play high school baseball through the American Legion league, where sports legend Phil Niekro coached him for two years. This picture was taken when Poppi came to Atlanta from Baton Rouge to watch Gip play ball. It was a thrill for Poppi to meet Niekro, one of his idols.

Gip also played on the CHHS football team as a wide receiver, which is where he met Chuck Scott, who was the position coach in charge of wide receivers. Coincidentally, Gip's jersey number, 40, had also been Chuck's professional jersey number. It was here that these two began a lifelong friendship.

Gip with Richard and me at Football Senior Night at CHHS. This is the traditional night when, at half time, senior players are introduced individually. Each player's football history and accolades from their four years of playing football are described. It's the night that each player gets his chance to be in the spotlight.

Gip, Richard, and me with Coach Chuck Scott at a high school football banquet, where Coach presented Gip with a football achievement award.

As if Gip wasn't busy enough with sports, holding down a job, and keeping a B average in school, he also loved hunting. Richard and Gip bonded through a shared love for hunting, and even when they came home empty-handed they'd be happy from enjoying the outdoors and spending time together. This photo was taken as the two set out for a deer hunt in the fall of Gip's senior year.

Our family had enjoyed several snow-skiing vacations at Winter Park, Colorado, and on this trip we decided to have our portrait taken at the top of the mountain. Because of Gip's athleticism and love of sports, snow skiing was another of his favorite pastimes.

For spring break of Gip's senior year, we took a family trip to the Grand Canyon. This was our last family vacation before Gip went to college—and before everything changed for our family.

Gip's high school senior portrait, full
of all the promise that lay ahead.

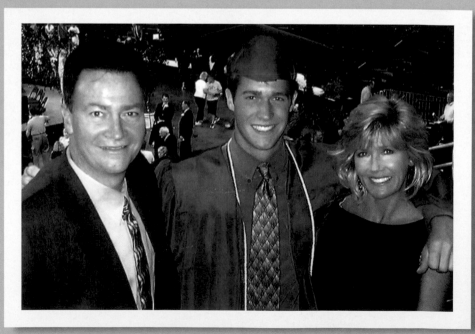

Gip with Richard and me just after his high school graduation ceremony.
Many family members and other loved ones came to see Gip graduate, and
we celebrated for the entire weekend!

CHAPTER 1

Saturday

Saturday, the sixth of September, started out like most Saturdays for our family. We got up, had our morning coffee, and were off to the races with our regular weekend routines. Fall was in the air, football mania was upon us, and we were pumped. Both boys had played sports throughout their youth, and football was quite a passion for our entire family. My husband, Richard, was headed to our son's school, Collins Hill High School, to paint our beloved Eagle mascot in the center of the football field. This had been a Saturday tradition for the past four years while our older son, Gip, played high school football. Our younger son, Taylor, was just entering his freshman year, and we were gearing up for another four years of football fun.

Through their Little League years, Richard coached both Gip and Taylor in football and baseball. Once they reached high school, Richard transitioned his role to parent and spectator, but he continued to offer coaching to our sons—discreetly of course—between quarters and innings. He also remained involved with their sporting careers through booster clubs, helping wherever dads were needed. He loved being with other parents, all of them working together making the field just right for their boys.

As Richard left the house that morning full of caffeine, carrying painting supplies, and with excitement in his eyes, he kissed me goodbye, hugged Taylor, and told us he loved us. We replied with the same, and we all went about our day with joyful hearts for the great promise of all that lay ahead.

This was an exciting time for our family: we were all in a good place. Gip had just left home a few weeks earlier for his freshman year of college. Taylor was starting his freshman year of high school. Richard had begun a new home-building career a few months earlier, and business was starting to boom. And me? Well, I was headed back into the work force after being home raising the boys for almost twenty years. I'd always held part-time jobs through the years to help make ends meet, but with college expenses ahead, I was going back to my pre-mom career. I had just landed my dream job in interior design and started working that very week. I was thrilled for the opportunities ahead for *all* of us.

After breakfast, Taylor and his friend Kurt went upstairs to play video games. I could hear them chattering about their upcoming high school football careers. They had high hopes of beating all their rival schools. Their laughter rippling through our home was music to my ears.

With a smile on my face I, too, began my Saturday ritual. I ran a few errands that morning, came home at midday, and started cleaning the house, all the while talking to my mom on the phone as I folded laundry, unloaded the dishwasher, and made up beds. We were having one of our weekend marathon-visiting calls, catching up on all the family's activities.

Mom called to check on me, wondering how I was holding up now that Gip, her first grandchild, was away at college. I was missing him, of course, but that was to be expected.

This was life in the right order, a day we all prayed for. We were aware that many changes and challenges lay ahead for our son, but emotions aside, we were prepared for this day, and so was he. Gip was a well-rounded young man through his involvement in school, sports, church, and youth groups. That was our saving grace.

We were excited about this new chapter in our son's life. But my mom knew I was going through withdrawal, as most parents do when their kids go off on their own for the first time. Of course the term "on their own" is quite a stretch. The reality is that they leave home, taking off on that magic carpet ride that mom and dad are still paying for—and praying for. Magically they're on their own and having the ride of their lives. At least, that's how it was *supposed* to be.

As I was putting away linens upstairs, still on the phone with my mother, I heard Richard rush into the house screaming my name. I told Mom I had to go and quickly hung up the phone. Even in that split second as I flew down the stairs, I knew something was terribly wrong.

CHAPTER 2

God No!

Moving day at college!

Just three weeks into his freshman year at the University of West Georgia in Carrollton, Gip was invited to go dove hunting in Vidalia, Georgia, by a new friend, a fraternity brother he'd met a week earlier. We
spoke with Gip on Friday night before the Saturday hunt, and he was very
excited. When Richard asked about hunter safety, Gip's friend assured
him there was no need for concern, explaining that it was a private hunt
on a relative's property with men who had been hunting all their lives.

"Be careful, son," Richard said to Gip.

"Don't worry, Dad. They're all experienced hunters. We'll be fine."
Those were Gip's last words to Richard that night.

The following morning, they headed to the hunting field. It was the first
day of dove season, and everyone was looking forward to it. They settled into
their positions and began the wait. Shortly after, they spotted a few doves
coming in over the trees from the left side. As Gip's friend raised his gun, he
accidentally fired too soon. He shot our son in the head with a twelve-gauge

semiautomatic shotgun round from approximately twenty-six feet away. The entire right front corner of Gip's skull was crushed from the blast. It hit him in the temporal area, just above his ear, near the top of his head.

His body slumped over, and he began to fall forward. His friend ran to him screaming, "I shot him! I shot him! I shot him!" When he rolled Gip over, Gip was completely unresponsive. The right side of his face was covered with bird shot. Already a pool of blood was beginning to form around his head. Hundreds of pellets had penetrated through his skull and into his brain.

Within seconds, other hunters in the field began rushing toward them. One of the first hunters to aid Gip was a preacher who started praying over our son right away. Another was a volunteer fireman; thanks to his emergency training, he was able to give Gip the "first response" medical care he needed. Gip was losing a tremendous amount of blood at a rapid pace. They worked feverishly to cover his skull, trying to hold back the bleeding.

One hunter had a cell phone and actually got a signal. That was rare, as this hunting field is in the middle of nowhere, and typically no signal was available. He called 911. Despite their remote location, the ambulance reached them in fewer than ten minutes. The official incident report shows the time of the accident as 12:26 p.m.

Upon their arrival, EMS crew members immediately began working on Gip; they had no time to waste. Things were grim, and everyone there knew it. We were told later that despite all the blood, they could see that Gip's eyes were open. One hunter reported how eerie it was to witness such a sight. He said it was as if Gip was looking at them, begging them to help him. Perhaps he was.

Just before the ambulance drove off, the sheriff quickly slipped Gip's phone out of the pocket of his hunting pants. He then scrolled through the phone address list looking for family phone numbers and found "Dad's cell." He made the gut-wrenching call, the kind no law officer ever wants to make and no parent ever wants to receive.

By this time, it was nearly 12:45 p.m. When the call came, Richard was across the football field, nowhere near his phone. Our friend Curtis answered when it rang. The voice on the other end was strong and stern asking for Mr. Richard Gayle. It was clear by his tone this was a serious matter. Curtis immediately shouted to Richard to answer the phone, saying that it "sounded important." Richard ran across the field, grabbed the phone and said "Hello?"

"Mr. Gayle, this is the Vidalia sheriff. Your son's been shot in a hunting accident. You need to get here immediately!"

"What? Is he all right? What happened? Where is he?" Already a million thoughts were racing through Richard's mind.

The sheriff responded hesitantly. Bound by legal issues and privacy protection laws, he was not allowed to divulge much information. Slowly he replied, "All I can say is that the ambulance just left the hunting field with your son, and it's *very* critical. They're taking him to Meadows Regional Medical Center here in Vidalia."

With his heart pounding, Richard, barely able to speak, replied, "I'm on my way now. How bad is it? Where was he shot?"

The sheriff once again hesitated, saying he could not disclose any details of the shooting. Richard's body was quivering by this time as he said, "Please, as a dad, I'm begging you—tell me about my son!"

In a compassionate tone, the sheriff replied, "I'm sorry, Mr. Gayle, but I'm afraid I can't tell you what part of his body was shot or how it happened." He paused for a second and said, "You need to get down here right away, sir, right away!"

For a moment Richard stood there, almost paralyzed with fear. Friends had already gathered around trying to understand what was going on based on Richard's end of the conversation. They tried to help, begging him to let them drive him home so he could get there safely. But in his state of shock, Richard took off running across the football field and headed to the parking lot. He was desperately trying to get home to me and rush to the hospital. In his frantic state, he dropped his keys several times as he scrambled to unlock his truck. Finally, he got the key in the door, hopped in, and raced to our house.

As Richard was speeding home, the ambulance was rushing Gip to the local hospital in Vidalia. The emergency room physicians began treating him as soon as he arrived, inserting a breathing tube to allow air to reach his lungs. They did their best to protect the hole in his skull, trying to prevent further blood loss. But the medical team knew right away they were not equipped to handle the severity of such injuries. Immediately, they called for a life-flight helicopter to airlift our son to the nearest Level One Trauma Center, located a couple of hours away in Savannah, Georgia.

The life-flight crew had just been informed about a heavy tropical storm coming in from the state of Florida. But when the radio dispatcher described the patient's dire medical condition—*nineteen-year-old-male, gunshot wound to the head, massive blood loss, unresponsive and in shock, patient needs Level One trauma care immediately*—the pilot, Dan Foulds, the life-flight nurse, Alison Herrington, and the paramedic, Jeff Clifton, realized they were Gip's *only* chance for survival. With a small window of opportunity, they looked at each other and agreed: They *had* to go. Despite the risks, they took off to save our son's life, putting their own in jeopardy by doing so.

As Richard drove home, desperately trying to figure out how he was going to tell me about Gip, his phone rang again. This time it was a nurse at the Vidalia hospital. She got Richard's phone number from the sheriff, who told her he'd already instructed the dad to go the Vidalia hospital. The nurse quickly called Richard to redirect him to Memorial University Medical Center, the site in Savannah to which they were airlifting our son. She gave Richard the hospital phone number so he could call from the road to check on Gip.

Richard continued to ask questions about Gip's status, but legalities prevented her, too, from providing much information. Richard pleaded with her, saying "This is my son we're talking about. Please tell me he's going to be all right."

There was silence on the other end of the phone. Richard continued, "You don't understand. I'm on my way home to tell my wife. I've got to give her something to hold on to. Please, give me *something!*"

Richard could hear her struggling to catch her breath. She was clearly upset and unable to respond. He continued to question her: "Where was he shot? How far is this other hospital? Is he stable enough to make the flight?"

She did her best to speak calmly, but the situation was grave, and there weren't many ways to phrase it. She told Richard she wasn't allowed to say what part of his body had been shot or comment on whether she thought he would survive the life flight. Her voice quavered as she told Richard how sorry she was and how they had done everything they possibly could to help our son.

When Richard arrived at our house, he rushed in screaming my name. "Beth! Beth! Where are you?"

I flew down the stairs. As I reached the bottom step, Richard was rounding the hallway corner to meet me. He grabbed me in a desperate embrace and gasped for air as he struggled to say, "Gip's been hurt."

I pulled away from him, looking for hope in his eyes, but he wouldn't look at me. I knew then it was critical. Already, I was struggling to breathe. Horrified, I whispered, "What happened?"

Richard clutched my shoulders and pulled me back into his arms. I could feel his heart pounding faster and faster. He choked as he uttered the gut-wrenching words, "Oh Baby, he's been shot. Gip's been shot!"

My knees buckled, and I began to fall. Richard tried to hold me up, but we both fell to the floor. I finally forced the unimaginable question from my lips, "But, but, he's still alive, right?"

Richard tried to stay calm, an impossible feat. He began breaking into a sweat. His reply was barely audible when he said, "He was alive when the life-flight crew picked him up. They're airlifting him to a Level One Trauma Center in Savannah right now. That's where we have to go, and we need to leave right away." He paused and whispered, "I *have* to believe that he's still alive . . . we both have to believe that."

With that he quickly lifted me up saying, "We've got to go! We need to get Taylor and get on the road."

Panic began to set in. "Oh, no. What are we going to tell Taylor?" I asked.

Doing his best to keep it together, Richard whispered, "We're telling him that Gip's been hurt in a hunting accident and we're going to the hospital to check on him. Nothing more, nothing less."

I quickly grabbed my purse and keys and called out to Taylor. He knew by my tone it was urgent and rushed down the stairs. We told him Gip was hurt in a hunting accident and we needed to get to the hospital. He raced upstairs to grab his tennis shoes. His friend came down with him with a somber look on his face; he knew it was bad. We told him to call his mom for a ride home and ask her to call everyone she knew to pray for Gip.

With no time to waste, we were on the road by 1:15 p.m. As we pulled out of the driveway, the three of us held hands and prayed for God to be with Gip, and with us, as we drove to him. We had not told Taylor that we didn't know if Gip was still alive or not. So after we prayed out loud with Taylor, Richard and I continued to hold hands, silently praying that our son was still alive. I can remember my exact prayer, "Oh dear God, please let him live. Please, please, please place your healing hands upon our son."

During that unbearable five-hour drive to Savannah, we called everyone we knew, begging them to pray for our son's survival. We asked them to go to their churches and fall to their knees, call their family and friends, and contact their pastors, priests, and ministers. We knew our only hope was prayer.

We called the Savannah hospital desperately trying to get information about our son, clinging to the hope that he was still alive. But due to the privacy protection laws, they, too, could provide little information. It was horrible! Finally, after nearly an hour, my father, a physician in Louisiana, got through to Dr. Louis Horn, Memorial University Medical Center's chief neurosurgeon, who was in touch with the life-flight crew and was preparing for Gip's arrival. He told my dad that Gip was still alive, but things were critical—very critical.

Dad called right away to let us know what was going on. I answered his call. At first he insisted on talking only to Richard. "Just put Richard on the phone," he demanded.

I was crying and pleading with him. "Daddy, I can't. He's driving. Please tell me Gip is still alive!"

"Yes honey, he's alive," he answered slowly.

I screamed with relief: "He's alive! He's alive! Thank you, Lord, he's alive!"

Then I asked, "Where was he shot? Did they tell you what part of his body was shot?"

I could hear Dad scrambling on the other end of the phone, trying to figure out just how he could tell his little girl such horrific news. He was desperately searching for the right words, but there were none.

Painfully, he whispered, "His head, sweetheart. Gip was shot in the head."

Richard and Taylor were desperately waiting to hear my dad's reply. As much as I couldn't bear to repeat what I'd just heard, I knew I had to. I honestly don't know how I got those life-shattering words out of my mouth, but somehow I mumbled, "In the head. Gip was shot in the head."

No one said anything. It was as if we were in a trance; we simply couldn't breathe. Finally, we took a deep *breath* as we digested the horror of it all. Richard was very stoic. He grasped my hand as he nodded that it was going to be all right. He was trying to be strong for me and Taylor, but I knew his heart was shattered. So was mine.

My whole body started shaking as I slowly asked, "Oh Daddy, are they giving him any hope, any hope at all?

Dad's tone quickly changed as he said with great conviction, "We have God, honey. And with God, we *always* have hope. Do you hear me? We are *never* giving up hope. We are all going to pray for God's divine healing."

As soon as we hung up, I was back on the phone calling our pastor and family and friends informing them that Gip was still alive. About fifteen minutes later, my phone rang again. It was Dr. Horn, who had been given our phone number by my father. He informed us that Gip had arrived and survived the flight. He told us Gip had lost a lot of blood, but they were working to stabilize him as they prepped him for surgery. Dr. Horn was calm in his manner and tone, but the message was clear that things were grim.

I asked Dr. Horn if he was a believer. He said, "Yes." I asked him to please pray for Gip, and for himself and his surgical crew, before he operated. He promised he would. As horrifying as it all was, we were greatly comforted knowing that Gip was being prayed over in person, and by the doctor who would operate on him.

We still had more than three hours of driving before reaching Savannah. It was gut-wrenching to be on the road knowing that our son was in life-threatening surgery without us nearby. The time did not pass quickly.

We continued to pray, but silently and separately. My phone was ringing continually. Each time, I jumped, wondering if it was Dr. Horn. I tried to remain calm, but it was an impossible feat.

When we finally arrived at the Trauma Center, we drove up the circular-drive entrance and jumped out of our car, leaving it sitting in the patient drop-off area. We knew it was not an authorized parking zone, but we were in a panic. We rushed inside to the information desk.

By this time it was about 6:00 p.m. Frantically, we told the receptionist that our son had just arrived via life flight, and we needed to get to him immediately. They asked if we were "the parents of the boy who was shot." Hearing those words pierced our hearts, but we replied, "Yes."

The receptionist's assistant offered to move our car, and Richard quickly handed her the keys. Then the hospital aide jumped up and raced through the hallways, showing us the way. It felt like an eternity before we reached the neurosurgery floor.

We passed several nurses' stations along the way and could feel stares of sympathy as they watched us rush to our son. We later found out that the entire hospital had been made aware of Gip's accident, and all were told to watch for our arrival and guide us to the right place. It was an unusual case: a gunshot wound to the head, a teenager, a family coming in from out of town. News like that spreads fast, I guess.

Once we got to the Neuroscience Intensive Care Unit (ICU), the nurses told us that Gip was still in surgery. They kindly shared their sympathy and informed us that a hospital chaplain had given Gip his "last rites" just before surgery. This is an anointment of oils used to bless the sick, typically the dying. It was clear that Gip was not expected to survive. Richard, Taylor, and I seemed unable to move at first. The nurse then directed us to the Neuroscience ICU waiting room and told us the doctors would come to that room as soon as the surgery was over.

At that point, we had no choice but to wait. We walked into the waiting area and began scanning the crowded room, searching for a place we could all sit together. Richard pointed to the corner of the room and motioned for us to sit there. Slowly we trudged over and more or less fell into the chairs. I happened to fall into the chair between Richard and Taylor. At first the three of us just stared into space, as if we had no thoughts at all. After a few minutes, Richard grabbed my hand, and I grabbed Taylor's. There was no eye contact between us, but we bowed our heads and prayed silently—together, but separately.

For several hours, Taylor was completely silent; we all were. Even at the tender age of fourteen, he knew this was not the time for questions. He knew we didn't have answers. I watched his lips move as he prayed for his brother. He was amazingly calm. He was letting God handle it—he was being Taylor. But I knew he was scared.

We tried to comfort each other with an occasional hand squeeze or a slight nod of "it's going to be all right." But it was tough, and our body language screamed fear. After a while, I gently put my arm around Taylor and held him like I was never going to let go. Seconds later, Richard leaned over, reaching out as far as he could and placed his arm around Taylor and me. We spoke no words. Each of us was immersed in our own heartache, not wanting to burden the other with our brokenness.

As time passed, we watched doctor after doctor come in to talk with other families about their loved ones. Not knowing what Gip's doctor looked like, we rose from our seats each time a different doctor walked in. Our hearts were pounding as we waited to hear them call out a family name. Typically one doctor walked in at a time and spoke with the patient's family in the waiting room in front of the other families.

After nearly three hours, a team of doctors and surgical assistants came around the corner and headed toward the waiting room as the clock edged toward 9:00 p.m. Exhaustion and despair consumed each one's face. I turned to Richard and whispered, "Oh dear God, that's them. Look at their faces. Those are Gip's doctors. God, help us!"

"The Gayle family?" they asked as they entered the waiting room.

We could hardly breathe, but Richard somehow managed to raise his hand as he struggled to get to his feet. Barely audible, he said, "We're the Gayles. Is, is, is our son all right?"

They gave no verbal response as they quickly escorted us down the hallway to a private room. Their body language made it clear they were not going to talk with us in front of other families. Richard held Taylor and me up as we walked trembling down what seemed like an endless hallway.

Once in the room, Dr. Horn told us Gip had survived the surgery but that things were critical. The blast had destroyed his brain's entire right frontal lobe, with the impact causing bruising and injury to the rest of his brain as well. The surgeons removed a substantial part of his crushed skull to allow for swelling. Damage was so extensive that permanent, crippling brain damage seemed inevitable. Dr. Horn phrased it delicately, but we grasped what he meant.

These doctors spent close to five hours in surgery, working diligently to save our son's life. There were so many concerns to address; I can't imagine what they must have felt. If not for their brilliance and expertise, Gip would not have survived the night.

Hundreds of birdshot pellets lay embedded in his skull and brain. The doctors carefully removed as many as possible. But because it was dangerous to dig too deep, countless pellets were left behind. There were grave concerns on multiple levels, but they were determined to do everything they could to give Gip a fighting chance. Even then, they knew it might not be enough.

Dr. Horn tried to offer us glimmers of hope but had to be honest. The harsh truth was that Gip might not make it through the night. And if he did, the damage was severe. The doctors said that for every hour Gip held on, his chances of surviving the next hour increased dramatically. But that was about as much hope as they could give us. It was grave, and we all understood that.

As they wrapped up their talks with us, Dr. Horn said that he and his staff would continue monitoring Gip and give us hourly updates. He informed us that it would be several more hours before we would be allowed to see our child.

My lips quivered as I asked Dr. Horn, "Did you pray for our son and yourselves before surgery?"

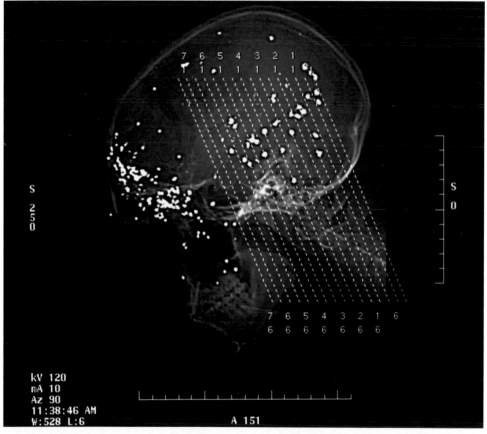

A CT scan showing the birdshot pellets.

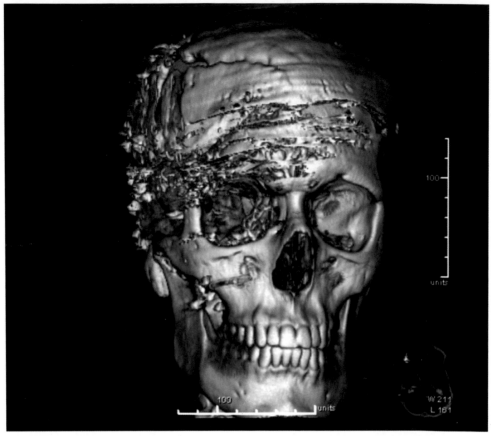

A CT scan showing the damage to Gip's skull.

"We *all* prayed," he said.

The rest of the surgical team added nods of assent that they, too, had prayed for our son.

Dr. Horn's physician assistant, Angela Winn, reached out to hug me as she said, "I prayed throughout the surgery asking for God's guiding hand."

We asked a few more questions, and then I hugged Dr. Horn and each team member. As Richard shook their hands thanking them for all their efforts, I wrapped myself around Taylor and held him as tightly as I could. We sat enveloped in each other's arms and wept.

As Dr. Horn reached for the door to leave, Richard said to him, "Doc, you don't know my son, but he's got the heart of a lion, and he *will* fight for his life." Richard took a deep breath and went on to plead, "Please, if you'll do everything you can to help him, he'll battle back. I know he will, I just know he will!"

Dr. Horn turned and said, "Mr. Gayle, he's going to need that heart. But I promise I'll do everything I can to help your son." He looked down for a moment, probably to regain his composure, and then looked straight into our eyes as he said, "I wish I had better news for you and your family. I wish I could give you something, medically, to give you hope."

He paused again, took the surgical cap off his head, and slowly ran his fingers through his hair as he said, "I have prayed, and I will continue to pray for your son. I believe God's medicine is much stronger than ours. So keep your faith strong, and I'll keep doing my part."

As the door closed behind Dr. Horn, my heart sank. Richard, Taylor, and I sat for a few minutes, stunned and speechless, our bodies slumped in the seat cushions. Hundreds of thoughts were racing through our minds. Knowing that Gip might not survive the night and fearing what he might have to face if he did survive . . . well, it was all too much to handle.

I wept as I turned to Richard and quietly whispered in his ear, "What do we pray for now? I don't want our child to suffer."

Richard turned to me, firmly grabbed my shoulders, and said, "We are praying for a miracle! Do you hear me? That is what we are praying for. And we're going to pray with conviction."

And so we did.

CHAPTER 3

Our New Journey

Beyond Recognition

It was another two hours before we were allowed to see Gip. He was in the Neuroscience ICU in a coma and was being monitored closely by several attendants. When the nurse came to get us, she told us we would have to be very quiet and could see our child for only a few minutes. She walked Richard, Taylor and me into the ICU area and pointed to Gip's unit: Number 10. We pulled the curtain open and eased our way in but were shocked to see a stranger in the bed. We rushed out to the nurse's station to report we had been sent to the wrong unit.

The head nurse heard us and quickly came around the corner to handle things personally. She apologized for the confusion, glanced at the information on the computer, and walked down to the unit. In less than a minute, she emerged from behind the curtain reciting Gip's full name and birth date as noted on his hospital ID wristband and chart. Stunned and confused, we crept back in.

Our bodies sank with disbelief at the sight before us. Taylor looked at Gip again, turned to us, and mumbled, "I'm telling you, they're wrong. That is not my brother."

Nothing could've prepared us for what we saw when we walked into that little ICU cubicle. It's an image we're still trying to erase from our minds and hearts to this day. Had we known what we were going to see, I don't think we would have taken Taylor in with us. Of course at the time, we couldn't think clearly about anything we were doing. When the nurse came to get us, we jumped up and followed her to the ICU. We had no idea what lay behind that curtain.

Gip's head was so swollen, he was beyond recognition. His features were severely distorted and out of proportion. He barely looked human. He appeared to be a very elderly, very overweight man. His head was wrapped in surgical bandages, but we could still see most of his face. It was covered with dozens of holes from the scattered birdshot. The entire right side of his head had been sprayed with pellets from the top of his skull, down past his eye and ear. The spread pattern even included parts of his nose, chin, and neck.

His right eye was pulled down so low from the swelling that it was almost lower than his nostrils. The upper right area of his head was deeply sunken from the absence of skull. He was truly unrecognizable and certainly did not look like our handsome son Gip.

I wiped the tears from my eyes just long enough to see Gip's hands—hands I was unsure I would recognize—*but I did.* As I held his hand in mine, I turned to Richard and whispered, "It's him. It's Gip. These are his hands. Oh dear God, these are his hands."

At that moment, Taylor reached over and carefully held Gip's other hand, cautious not to touch any tubes or wires. With tears in his eyes, he bent down close to Gip's head and quietly whispered, "Don't worry, Gip, I've got your back. You hear me? You're gonna be all right, Gip. You're gonna be all right."

I thought Richard and I were going to absolutely lose it right then and there. It was a sweet, tender moment but so desperately sad at the same time.

All of a sudden, Gip's monitors began to sound. We had no idea what it meant. Nurses rushed in and began calling for help. Taylor turned around and left the room. I rushed out behind him. It was just too much to bear. We went back to our private waiting room. The nurses wouldn't allow Richard to stay either, so he soon joined us.

Now What?

As the three of us sat in that tiny little room trying to process what we had just seen, I knew we needed help. Barely able to breathe, let alone talk, I somehow managed to call my mom and a few friends to update them on Gip's condition and plead for their prayers. They quickly spread the word to others for a pyramid of prayer.

While I made phone calls, Richard put his arm around Taylor and whispered that we were going to make it through this. Taylor was silent but nodded in agreement. He clasped his hands tightly as he bowed his head. For the next couple of hours, we stared at the floor through tear-filled eyes. Every now and then Richard would lean over, offering a few words of comfort. But for the most part, little was said.

Suddenly there was a knock on the door. Richard jumped up and opened it. A man stood in the doorway asking if we were the Gayle family. We assumed he was someone with the hospital medical staff, so Richard quickly asked, "Is Gip all right?"

The man took a deep breath and said "I'm um, I'm um . . . well, my son is the one who shot your son. We came as soon as we heard. I'm so sorry. We're all so sorry."

Richard reached out, put his hand on the man's shoulder, and said, "I know this must be very difficult for you, too. We appreciate you coming." Richard then motioned for him to have a seat and said, "We haven't heard anything about what happened to our son. Can you tell us what happened?"

The father looked down, rubbed his head, and told us he had not been at the hunting field, so he didn't know all the details either. He looked up and said, "All I know is that it was a terrible accident. They were dove hunting, and somehow my son accidentally shot your son in the head."

I rose from our sofa and sat beside his chair. I put my arm around him and said, "This is a nightmare for both of our families." I began to shake as I said, "Is your son here? I want to tell him not to worry."

"Yes. He's outside in the hallway, with my wife," he replied.

It was obvious this father was taken aback by our reaction. But how else would we respond? This was a horrible accident, and everybody involved was in unbearable pain. This was a place for peace, not poison.

We walked out of the waiting room to meet the young man who shot our son. As we approached him, he stood very still and made no eye contact. It was clear that he was in shock. We all were. Richard and I reached out and hugged him and his mom. I reached for his hand and encouraged him to be strong and to pray hard. He seemed unable to respond. I told him that we would all get through this together. We then thanked him and his parents for coming.

And Then Came the Angels

While talking with this family, we noticed that the hallway was rapidly crowding with young men and women, more than thirty of them. We didn't know who they were, so we began to move to the side of the hall to allow them to pass. But they quickly informed us that they were there to be with *us*—that they were Gip's brothers. Gip had been in college for only three weeks when this accident happened, but already he had made quite a few wonderful friends. Most of the kids were from his fraternity, Chi Phi. It was a long drive from their college to Savannah, but that didn't stop them from coming. One by one, they introduced themselves, and one by one we tearfully hugged them, bowled over by their presence.

After the introductions, we asked if they would pray with our family. Without hesitation, they lined up in the hallway hand in hand. It was an awesome sight to behold as they filled one long hallway and overflowed into the next. Each one spoke from deep within his heart as he prayed out loud for his brother. One young man cried out, "Lord, we're asking for a miracle. Please hear our prayer." Another spoke up saying, "God, you are the Great Physician with the power to intercede . . . please intercede and spare our brother's life." Some held their heads high, desperately trying to be strong, while others bowed down, overcome with emotion.

As they took turns praying for our son, we could feel God's presence surrounding us like a blanket of peace. Their words sent chills up and down our spines. Richard has said many times that he could sense Jesus walking those hospital hallways, preparing a miracle.

It's amazing how God works. Had we been asked if we wanted to be surrounded by kids we didn't even know, we would've told you "absolutely not!" We would've thought we needed to be by ourselves, alone in our misery to nurse our breaking hearts. But God knew better. No doubt, *He* sent those young men and women to be with us at that very moment to lift us in a way that only they could.

As we gathered in the waiting room, these kids warmed our hearts and raised our spirits. They told us one story after another of how Gip had already touched their lives with his humor and joyful spirit. Several young men and women said that Gip always had a smile on his face and was fun to be around because of it. One young man said that Gip was easy to talk to, and he already felt like they were bonding as brothers. Another friend, who had been struggling with career choices, asked Gip for guidance. Gip told him to take it to God in prayer and then follow His lead.

These young people stayed the night with us. Some slept on waiting-room sofas and chairs, while others sprawled on the cold tile floors in the hallways. It was like a revolving door for these precious young men and women. As some would leave to return to school, others would appear to replace them.

Led by Kyle Standridge and Eric "Fathead" Thomason, these wonderful fraternity brothers put together a fund-raiser to help with our family's emergency expenses. We felt abundantly blessed by their outpouring of love and support. We've thanked them many times for being there for us, but I don't think they will ever truly know the magnitude of what their presence meant to our family.

Divine Confirmation

Not surprisingly, we weren't trying to sleep during this time of crisis. But as the wee hours approached, we inadvertently closed our eyes from time to time out of sheer exhaustion. At one point, Richard even dozed off and had a dream . . . a deep, consuming dream.

In it, Richard saw Jesus leaning over the hospital bed with His hand gently placed over the right side of Gip's skull. Suddenly a beautiful glow appeared around Gip's head as if a heavenly light were surrounding it. Jesus looked up for a moment and then looked over at Richard and smiled.

Richard woke up and jumped straight off the couch. He quickly sat back down, rubbed his eyes, and held his head in his hands. I was startled by his sudden movements and asked what was wrong. He leaned over and whispered his dream in my ear. He said the image was clearer than anything he had ever seen before. This was very unusual because in the thirty years I've known Richard, he's rarely been able to recall a dream. But this one, he did. Sometimes we wonder if it really was a dream.

Neither of us had ever had an experience like that, so we were both shaken. We chose to believe it was a message from God that He was with our son. For us, it was a firm reminder—divine confirmation, if you will—that God is the Great Physician and that indeed it was *His* healing powers at work. It helped us refocus on just who was in charge.

All Is Well—"Mama and Them" Are Here

Richard and I grew up in Baton Rouge, Louisiana, but have lived just outside Atlanta, Georgia, for the past two decades. Over the years, much of our extended family moved from Louisiana and became scattered across the United States. Once they were called about Gip's accident, they all took flights to Savannah.

I don't care how old we get or how grown up we think we are; when a crisis comes along, we want our parents.

I felt badly for Richard because his mom, Mimi, had passed away a few years earlier. He certainly could have benefited from her loving presence at such a time as this. Sadly, his dad could not be there either because his poor health left him unable to travel. Richard had always been very close to his father, so it was tough not having him nearby. Because of their special bond, we had named our first son after Richard's dad, Gipson, also nicknamed "Gip" and often referred to as "the Gipper," just as our son came to be.

Thankfully both my parents were able to come to Savannah. The moment they walked into the waiting room, we practically fell into their arms. Richard is very close to my mom and dad as well. So he, too, felt the comfort of their parental presence.

Richard's only sibling, Jeanette, and her husband, Camille, were unable to travel as well. They ached to be with us, but Jeanette had just undergone extensive leg surgery and was off her feet for six weeks.

I am blessed to be one of six children, and we're all very close at heart. Unfortunately, we live in different states now. But each one came to Savannah as soon as the news reached them. They flew in from Louisiana, Oklahoma, Texas, and Tennessee. I cannot describe how much it meant having them all there. Being surrounded by family made it seem bearable.

Already we were bombarded with issues that had to be dealt with fairly quickly. Medical decisions had to be made; health insurance questions were starting to surface; Taylor's absence from school was a concern; our dog had been left alone at home, and much more. But from the moment my family arrived, they took control of the chaos that surrounded us.

My older brother, Tate, could lead a nation in his sleep if he had to! So when he got there, he began issuing marching orders, and everyone lovingly and willingly stepped up to the plate to help.

Because of the emergent situation, the office staff did not approach us for Gip's health insurance information when we first arrived. But they needed this data to enter him into their hospital system. So later that night, a hospital representative came to the waiting room asking if we had Gip's health insurance card.

We didn't. Since he was taken to the hospital via life flight, we did not know where his clothes or personal belongings were. I told the hospital attendant I did not have Gip's card, then handed her *my* health insurance card, explaining that Gip's insurance information matched mine, except that his member ID code was JC.

The entire waiting room fell silent. Even people who didn't know us turned their heads. The hospital rep took a step back, put her hand over her heart, and asked, "JC?" Out of all the possibilities, Gip's ID letters were JC. Of course we were all thinking the same thing: Jesus Christ. It seems a bit crazy, I know, but we took this as yet another one of God's little signs reminding us that Jesus Christ was in charge.

Later, someone brought in a sack filled with Gip's belongings from the hunting field. I reached for it thinking Gip's insurance card might be there. None of us knew the horror that lay within that bag.

I opened it and almost passed out at the sight of Gip's clothes, torn apart and covered in blood. In an effort to save our son's life, paramedics had to hurriedly rip Gip's clothes to medically tend to him.

Once my brother Tate realized what was in the bag, he quickly grabbed it from me and bolted from the room. Sifting through the rest of the items, Tate found Gip's wallet, cell phone, and truck keys. He cleaned it all off and put it in a safe place. He then took Gip's insurance card to the hospital office, and I never had to see those bloody clothes again.

CHAPTER 4

Prayer Power

From the very beginning, Gip was covered in prayer. From the men on the hunting field to the life-flight crew to the hospital surgeons and on to our family and friends, Gip's needs were being lifted. Our home church as well as other local churches and prayer ministries were praying nonstop for Gip and our family.

Just hours after Gip's accident, during the Saturday evening service, one of our pastors, Father Eric Hill, walked to the altar and stood with his back to the congregation. This was very unusual. Within minutes, complete silence fell upon the room as everyone waited for him to turn around. But he stood with head bowed, shoulders slumped, and hands clasped tightly. Friends said they could hear him praying but couldn't make out what he was saying. Unsure what to do, everyone sat quietly in their pews, wondering what was happening.

Finally, he turned around. It was clear he was overcome with grief. He looked up and said that a church member was in great need of prayer. He paused for a moment as he gathered his composure, then reported that he had just spoken with the Gayle family and that Gip had been shot in the head in a hunting accident a few hours earlier and was not expected to survive the night. He asked everyone to bow their heads. Teary-eyed, he led them in prayer for our child. I have tears in my eyes right now just thinking about it.

Chuck Scott, Gip's high school football coach, who was also his Christian youth group mentor with Young Life (YL), a worldwide Christian outreach program, was instrumental in implementing the "prayer power" Gip so desperately needed. When he first heard about the accident, he started sending emails to get prayers flowing as quickly as possible. Through phone calls and emails, Chuck developed a "prayer-warrior team" for Gip.

Within hours, hundreds of people were forwarding Chuck's emails to *their* family and friends and so on. Soon, people all over the world were hearing about Gip's accident and Chuck's prayer team quickly grew be-

Gip receiving an award from his high school football coach, Chuck Scott, at the Collins Hill High School football banquet.

yond measure. Before we knew it, thousands were praying for our son. I truly believe it was that prayer power that carried our family through those difficult times.

Chuck's emails kept everyone updated on Gip's ever-changing condition so they could pray specifically for each need. At one point, Chuck's list had grown so large that his AOL Internet provider shut him down for "spamming," sending to too many people at one time.

Once Chuck realized what was happening, he contacted AOL and spoke to a manager to explain Gip's situation. When Chuck told her that he was Gip's Young Life leader and needed to keep this prayer power going, the manager gasped as she shared that she had been in YL herself and it had truly blessed her life. She quickly pulled some strings and put Chuck's emails back in business. He was given an official spam account with AOL, just to keep Gip's prayer warriors on bended knees. How about *that* for divine intervention?

As I sat in the Savannah chapel, I stared at the stained glass window and wept. I prayed that God would give our family the strength to make it through the next few hours. I prayed for Gip's survival, I prayed for a miracle. As I begged God to hear my prayers, the door in the back of the chapel opened and within seconds, I heard piano music accompanied by what sounded like the voice of an angel—a beautiful male tenor voice singing out the name of Jesus. The only word to the song was the name of Jesus. As the young man finished singing, I walked to the back and introduced myself. This amazing voice belonged to a porter at the hospital who was on his break and said he felt the need to sing and praise God. I knew then this was God in all His kindness whispering to me through this young man, offering a moment of peace in the midst of so much agony. I cannot put into words how I felt; it was a God moment! Our Father was faithful then and has been throughout our journey. We serve a powerful God!

—Richard Gayle Sr., Gip's father

Below is Chuck's very first email.

09/06/03

Dear Friends,

It is with a heavy heart that I send this urgent request. Gip Gayle, one of my former Young Life kids and football players, was shot in the head in a hunting accident this morning. He has gone through surgery and the doctors don't give him much of a chance to live.

Gip graduated last year and was the kid I was closest to at Collins Hill High School. He was my sons' (Chad and Caleb) favorite player and is one of their heroes in life. Please pray for Gip and his family. The comfort I find in all this is that Gip's heart belongs to Jesus. Gip brought all of his friends to Young Life club because he wanted them to know Jesus too. Please pray for God's leading as I will have some difficult times ahead with Gip's family and friends.

Thanks for caring.

Serving Christ together,

Chuck

Chuck is married and has three children and a full-time career but still found time to reach out and help Gip in every way he could. Having been in YL most of his life, Chuck has cultivated a huge following of Young Lifers all over the world, and they became instant prayer warriors for Gip. Chuck also has a wonderful circle of friends from his former football career. He keeps in touch with many teammates and coaches who joined forces to pray for Gip. Chuck played wide receiver at Vanderbilt University, where he earned All-SEC and All-America honors in 1983. He played as a professional for the Los Angeles Rams in 1986 and the Dallas Cowboys in 1987. He wanted to stay involved in football after his playing days, so he became a wide receiver coach at our local high school.

But Chuck's real passion has always been with youth ministry. His parents helped pioneer Young Life in Florida, where they established a YL camp and remained on staff for many years. Chuck's exposure to the amazing work and blessings of this ministry inspired him to choose this path for his lifetime career as well.

At first, Gip and Chuck built a relationship around their love for football and their *twisted* sense of humor, on and off the field. But their bond strengthened even more when Coach Chuck jokingly gave an ultimatum to his football players saying that they could either come to Young Life club or run extra laps after football practice. Gip went to YL club!

After Chuck sent his first email prayer request, he began calling a group of Gip's high school football buddies. He invited them to meet on the football field the following night to pray for Gip. Most of these kids were away at college. But many drove all the way home, met on the fifty-yard line, and took a knee.

With their heads bowed, Chuck led them in prayer. He told us you could've heard a pin drop, it was so quiet. Before they left, Chuck obtained many of their email addresses so he could send updates and continue to ask for their prayers.

When we heard about this prayer session on the football field, we were overwhelmed. Of course we were very grateful to Chuck for putting it together, but we were also quite moved to hear about Gip's friends caring enough to gather to pray for him. Thank you, young men.

CHAPTER 5

Footprints in the Sand

I t wasn't long before friends began arriving in Savannah. The hospital is about four and a half to five hours away from our home. We were over-whelmed to see so many come so far to be with us. As we stood to hug them, we wept with each embrace. Richard, Taylor, and I were amazed at this outpouring of love and support. Looking back, I can see God's handi-work in this whole procession of earthly angels, who came to carry us at a time when we were unable to carry ourselves.

After we'd spent the first night in the ICU waiting room, the hospi-tal staff was kind enough to offer us an empty patient room the following morning, giving us a place to freshen up a bit. The room happened to be in the maternity ward. As wonderful as it was to have a room and bath to ourselves, we were surrounded by families there to celebrate life through the birth of their child. And, well, we were there facing the looming threat of death—possibly losing our child. I have to admit, that was difficult.

Knowing we had left town with only the clothes on our backs, several friends gathered at our home to pack suitcases with clothes and a few per-sonal items we might need. The next day they arrived in Savannah with some of our belongings. It was such a gift to have something clean to change into, as we had been wearing the same clothes for several days.

While packing our things, our friends thought of something else we might want to have: photos of Gip. What a gift. They grabbed several pictures off our refrigerator and put them in a little bag. When they ar-rived in Savannah, they handed me the bag. I clutched my heart as I looked inside and saw pictures of my child in all his perfection, the way I remembered him. The way he used to be. The way I yearned for him to be again.

I wept as I held those photos close to my heart. Every chance I got, I found myself showing off our precious son to anyone who would look at the photos and bragging on him to anyone who would listen. It seemed to help even *me* remember Gip, the way he had been.

The nurses helped me tape some of the photos to the I.V. pole just above Gip's bed. I know it seems crazy, but it was really important to me that the medical staff and caregivers have a "visual" of exactly who had been placed in their care. I wanted them to know of the perfection hidden beneath all that swelling, behind all those pellet wounds, beyond all those tubes and monitors. This was *our child* lying in that hospital bed, fighting for his life.

Those were some really dark times. Every hour was critical, and we all knew it. We found ourselves staring at the large round clock hanging on the waiting room's back wall. Its hands seemed to move in slow motion from one number to the next. We were painfully aware of each passing second.

The fear was gripping, as it permeated our minds and bodies and filtered deep into our souls. We didn't know how to process such devastation. This was heartache we'd never known . . . pain we'd never witnessed . . . helplessness we'd never felt. Our world was spinning out of control, and there was nothing we could do to stop it.

Family and friends continued to lift us in prayer and help in whatever way they could. Looking back, I can see there was only one set of "footprints in the sand." In that famous poem, only one set of footsteps showed because God was carrying his child. And in the same way, God had sent His earthly angels to carry us through our tough journey.

And carry us they did!

Footprints in the Sand

Last night I had a dream. I dreamed I was walking along the beach with the Lord. Across the sky flashed scenes from my life. For each scene, I noticed two sets of footprints in the sand: one belonged to me, the other to the Lord.

After the last scene of my life flashed before me, I looked back at the footprints in the sand. I noticed that at many times along the path of my life, especially at the very lowest and saddest times, there was only one set of footprints.

This really troubled me, so I asked the Lord about it. "Lord, you said that once I decided to follow you, You'd walk with me all the way. But I noticed that during the saddest and most troublesome times of my life, there was only one set of footprints. I don't understand why, when I needed You the most, You would leave me."

The Lord replied, "My precious child, I love you and I would never leave you. During your times of suffering, when you could see only one set of footprints, it was then that I carried you."

CHAPTER 6

Holding on to Hope

Can You Hear Us?

As hours passed, it seemed the first day just sort of rolled into the second day and then into the third. Gip remained comatose, so there were no obvious signs for us to know how he was. All we could do was try to interpret the nurses' facial expressions as they checked his vital signs and monitors every few hours. We stayed on a roller-coaster of emotions each day, wondering if our son was going to survive.

The doctors were in awe that Gip was able to endure the gunshot wound, let alone the life flight and the grueling five-hour surgery that followed. At that point, every hour he was still alive was considered a bonus.

Gip had so many tubes going in and out of him it was hard to tell what was doing what. It was overwhelming to hear all the beeps and see all the flashing lights. Even when things were somewhat stable, they still seemed chaotic to us. We found ourselves staring at the monitors, watching the numbers go up and down. Every little change brought us up and down. We jumped from our seats each time we heard a new noise or saw a new light. We finally had to force ourselves not to "monitor" the monitors.

The doctors did not want Gip overstimulated, so visits remained limited to five minutes every two hours. We counted the minutes between visits, anxiously waiting to be with him again. But for me, walking back into Gip's room was almost too much to handle. The horrific swelling, the birdshot pellets embedded in his face, and the many tubes going in and out of his body made it a tough sight to behold. Even though I couldn't bear to look at my son like that, I couldn't take my eyes off him either. It seemed easier to be strong when I was in the waiting room, away from this daunting visual.

With all the medical apparatus hooked to Gip, it was difficult to find a part of his body to touch. As a mom, I wanted to feel the warmth of my child's skin and for him to feel the warmth of mine. I wanted to rub his back and gently sing to him as I had done so many times when he was a little boy. I ached to communicate with him somehow and comfort him. I just had to let him know I was there with him. I carefully slid my hand over his and softly glided my fingers back and forth across his skin. With each stroke, my eyes watered and my heart prayed.

Obviously, with Gip in a coma, we didn't know if he could hear us talking or not. But that didn't stop us. Richard, Taylor, and I spoke softly as we continued to tell him how much we loved him and how proud we were of him. We encouraged him to stay strong . . . to fight . . . to pray.

We held Gip's hands as we held each other's and tearfully lifted him in prayer. We truly believe it raised Gip's spirits to hear our words of encouragement, to feel our presence, and to listen to our prayers. If nothing else, it helped us hold onto hope.

Oh Mama, Don't You Cry!

There were other mysterious happenings that helped us cling to hope. As my sister Helen was packing to come to Savannah on the night of the accident, she was praying fervently for Gip. When she went to sleep, naturally he was on her mind. The following day she remembered a remarkable dream where Gip came to her that night, woke her up, and asked for a favor.

"Aunt Helen, wake up. I need your help," he said.

"Sure, Gip, what do you need?" Helen asked.

"Tell my mom not to cry," Gip replied.

Helen sat up in bed and asked Gip what he meant.

"There's gonna be a miracle, Aunt Helen!" Gip paused for a moment and went on to say, "Tell Mom to take lots of pictures. She'll need them to tell about God's miracle."

He began to walk away, but then he turned around and said, "This is important, Aunt Helen."

Helen nodded, and Gip faded into the night.

Was this a dream? Well, it might appear that my family is dream-crazy, but we've never had these experiences before. I'm not sure how to react to all this myself. But the Bible does tell of many instances where dreams were used to communicate messages. So for us, we clung to the hope that a miracle *was* about to happen.

My sister Helen Darling is an accomplished singer and songwriter. Just before she left for Savannah, she met with her cowriter, Billy Montana. She told him about Gip's accident and about her dream. Together they began writing a song that is now called "Miracle."

When Helen arrived in Savannah, she brought her guitar and played her new song for our family and friends. Needless to say, there wasn't a dry eye in the place, including the doctors and nurses. The hospital staff loved it so

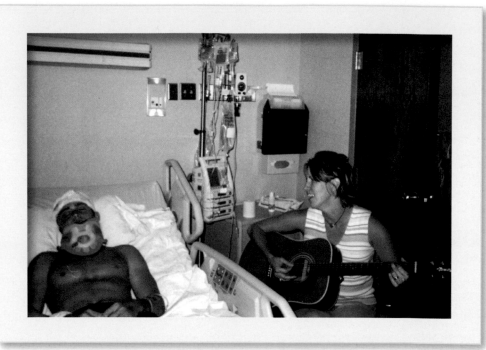

Gip's Aunt Helen singing "Miracle," the song she wrote for him immediately after his accident.

much they asked her to play her song for some of the other families, which she did.

The lyrics are beautiful and inspiring. The melody is breathtaking. And of course, in my humble opinion, my sister sang like an angel. The song's main line is "Oh Mama, don't you cry. It's gonna be all right. There's gonna be a miracle tonight."

And we continued to pray for one.

Miracle

Lyrics by Helen Darling and Billy Montana

Don't you think it's just like life to push you to the edge
To make you walk out on a wire without a net
We're living in a world of things we'll never understand
But maybe we don't need to know that much
Maybe sometimes love's enough

Oh Mama don't you cry . . . it's gonna be alright
There's gonna be a miracle tonight
So push your fears aside . . . and lift your hopes up high
Cuz there's gonna be a miracle tonight

I may be a traveler out on some broken road
But somehow I know I will find my way back home
And there'll be laughter in the backyard
As the leaves begin to fall
At least that's how it looks from here
So dry your eyes and save your tears

continued on next page

Oh Mama don't you cry . . . it's gonna be alright
There's gonna be a miracle tonight
So push your fears aside . . . and lift your hopes up high
Cuz there's gonna be a miracle tonight

Well forget those doubts . . . forget the odds
Let's just believe with everything we've got

Oh Mama don't you cry . . . it's gonna be alright
There's gonna be a miracle . . .
Push your fears aside . . . lift your hopes up high
Cuz there's gonna be a miracle tonight
Oh Mama won't it just be wonderful . . .
There's gonna be a miracle tonight

Cuz we're living in a world of things we'll never understand . . .

© 2012 Helen Darling and Billy Montana

CHAPTER 7

Getting Through It

When God Is All You Have

Watching Taylor weep as he stood bedside staring at his big brother just about ripped our hearts out. Despite our efforts to play up Gip's condition, Taylor knew how desperate things were; he could see it. He didn't realize it then, but he was fighting for *his* life, too, because life as he knew it was changed forever.

Prior to this incident, no matter what happened in our lives, Richard could find a way to fix it. If something was broken, Richard repaired it. If we needed advice or had to make a tough decision, Richard's wealth of wisdom shined the light. If we needed a hug, Richard's arms were open wide. He's been our earthly security blanket for whatever life threw at us. I never really thought about it much, but deep inside I guess I always counted on that.

But we'd just been stripped of every human safety net we'd ever had. And suddenly Richard, the love of my life, the strongest man I've ever known both spiritually and emotionally, was struggling with his role. He's the father, the head of the household, the man in charge. In his mind it's his job to take care of his family, his job to fix things. But this was different. How could he fix *this?*

My heart sank when I saw the man who was my rock overcome with despair. He had a lost look in his eyes I'd never seen before. From that moment on, that feeling of security we all once had was gone, and we felt bare without it.

I remember sitting next to Gip's hospital bed and looking across the room at my precious family, realizing our lives would never be the same. I recall thinking to myself, "How will we ever get through this?"

We are Christians, and we have our faith. But we were being tested beyond anything we'd ever imagined we would face. Like most people, we had never allowed ourselves to think of such tragedy occurring in our lives. I feared we weren't equipped to handle this level of devastation.

So how did we handle it? Well, we crumbled. Many times we crumbled. But we came to realize that even during this very critical time—even when we crumbled—we felt peace through prayer.

How could we be in such pain and yet feel such peace? I believe the answer to that question is "God." Throughout the Bible, He tells us to come to Him when we're weary and He will give us rest. He says He is our refuge in our time of need, our shelter from the storm. Well, we were certainly in a storm; we were weary and needed rest. So with every breath we took, we turned to Him in prayer. And it was "in that place," as we prayed without ceasing, that we found the peace needed to sustain us.

Our friends Elaine and Warren told us they were heartbroken as they drove to Savannah, fully expecting to walk into unbearable gloom and doom. They say they never experienced such hope in a place where despair seemed so imminent. Today, they often reminisce how moved they were by the undeniable peace they witnessed in that waiting room.

We weren't prepared for this crisis, but God was. And even though we didn't realize it at the time, He *did* equip us.

As our lives were unraveling, He revealed Himself to us through others, and somehow we found the strength to hold on. It was through those tough times we realized, more than ever before, that no matter what happens in our lives, God would get us through it.

To me, believing *that* is what faith really is.

One Day at a Time

For the first few days, Richard and I were literally numb, physically and emotionally. Our son's life was hanging in the balance. We sometimes didn't know where to put ourselves. No matter where we sat or stood, we seemed to be in the way of nurses or doctors as day and night they rushed in and out tending to our child's needs. It was mind-boggling to see how many medical issues they had to keep up with. Each hour seemed to bring a new concern.

The brain is the body's central control center, so an injury there affects everything else. For one thing, it regulates the body's temperature, and due to his severe infections Gip's temperature continued to spike out of control. This led to repeated shocks to his body's system. His heart rate was unstable as well, and that continued to be a serious concern. The swelling in his brain was linked to spinal-fluid buildup and erratic increases in brain pressure levels. Any one of these issues could be life-threatening for someone in such critical condition.

One surgically implanted device in particular monitored the ICP (intracranial pressure) levels in Gip's brain. As much as we tried not to look at any of his monitors, it was hard not to watch that particular one. After seeing how often the nursing staff checked its status, we sensed the serious implications of its numbers. We snuck glances at the monitor as often as we could without letting each other know we were looking. It became a bit of a cat-and-mouse game between Richard and me as we pretended not to look but reacted if the numbers were climbing. It was difficult to hide that level of fear.

As the doctors eased Gip off sedatives, they began performing sensory checks, looking for signs of neurological responses. We stood in the corner praying that Gip would respond. Tearfully we watched as they pinched his fingers, tickled his toes with a pin, spoke loudly to him, and used flashlights to check his pupils' reactions to light. These evaluations were done every couple of hours but all to no avail. It was difficult to watch them poke and prod our child to get a response from him, only to see him lie motionless.

Several times Taylor called Gip's name in hopes that Gip would hear him and respond. He got louder with each word as he said, "Gip, Gip, wake up. Please wake up, Gip."

We did our best to guard our hearts from the constant attacks of fear. But it wasn't easy. Our emotions were running rampant. There were many discussions about the odds Gip was facing and what we needed to prepare ourselves for. We were in complete overload. We asked the doctors a million questions about Gip's tomorrows. As much as they tried to sugarcoat their answers, the reality of Gip's situation was evident: He might not have many tomorrows.

That's when we realized we had to approach the situation with a one-day-at-a-time attitude. We could not continue to walk through that hospital door each hour as if we were watching our son die. So we decided we were going to watch him *live,* for as long as we had him with us.

That might sound very Pollyanna-ish, but it was much better to be thankful for each moment that we did have with our child than to focus on the moment we might not have him.

It wasn't easy, but as we worked on this attitude change, we grasped a much deeper meaning of the phrase "every day is a gift." Realizing this gift comes only one day at a time made us even more determined to appreciate it one day at a time. And that's how we got through it: one day at a time.

CHAPTER 8

Celebrate Every Blessing

A s we spent hour after agonizing hour praying for Gip's survival, we soon became focused on being thankful for every little sign of hope. Each time Gip's ICP levels improved, we felt great relief. When his temperature remained within normal range, we bowed our heads in thanks. When Gip's lungs were breathing clearly or if his vital signs were stable for even a few hours, we rejoiced. Whenever Gip wasn't moving backward, we celebrated that he was moving forward.

Some days our little victories weren't so small. Just three days after Gip's accident, in the late afternoon, the nurse rushed to the waiting room to tell us that Gip was showing slight movement in his right leg. We dashed into the ICU to see what was happening. Before this, Gip had shown no signs of deliberate movement anywhere on his body. We stood there as the nurse began prompting another response from Gip by slightly tickling his leg. Much to our surprise, it jumped. So of course, we jumped, too—for joy!

As the evening progressed, Gip slowly awoke from his coma. Although moving to physical stimulus prompts, he was still not responding to our auditory triggers, voice requests to move this or that. At that point, the doctors couldn't tell us if Gip was able to hear or not. The physical injury was to his head's right side, so our concern was great about sight or sound recovery on that side. But we still had hope for the left side, so we held on to that hope as best we could.

Gip's head was heavily bandaged and strapped into a head-and-neck brace to keep him stable. Unable to move his head, he couldn't respond to us with even a slight nod. He also had tubes in his throat and masks around his nose and mouth, so he couldn't verbally respond to us either. Moreover, his face was so swollen he was unable to open either eye.

Miraculously, by the third day's end, Gip began to respond to simple commands by squeezing our hands. He could hear us! That's when we knew that he knew we were at his side. The nurses were trying to give him verbal commands to continue testing his senses and levels of understanding. But I was so excited that he could hear; all I wanted to do was scream, "I love you, Gip!" That was what I wanted him to hear more than anything else. The commands could wait.

Because Gip had suffered such a severe head injury, his responses were not immediate. It took a long time for his brain to process the verbal command, send the message to his hand to squeeze, and then actually do it. We could see the anguish in his face as he struggled. It was difficult to watch our precious child fight so hard just to squeeze our hands. But he did it. So for that moment, asking Gip to squeeze our hands was the gift we asked for, received, and celebrated.

Gip continued to respond to our simple commands and questions by using the "squeeze once for yes and twice for no" system. We were all anxious for our turn to hold Gip's hand and say, "It's me, Gip. If you can hear me, please squeeze my hand." So many family members were with us that the nurse asked us to let Gip rest. She said his hand was probably hurting from all the squeezing, but he had no way to tell us. We let him rest while we returned to the waiting room and told everyone about the hand-squeezing marathon we'd just had with our son.

There's a humorous subplot underlying those hand-squeezing sessions. Gip has always been known for his firm handshake. He's a big believer in a robust handshake being an indicator of manhood. I'm not sure if Gip is famous or notorious for that, but people have commented on his vigorous handshake all his life. As he got older, he took great pride in it. So I can only imagine what he was thinking as we asked him to squeeze our hands. He probably worked harder than most patients to accomplish that task.

The doctors, in awe of Gip's unprecedented signs of recovery, were celebrating with our family. But they still cautioned us about his critical condition and other concerns that lay ahead. While working with him on following commands, we noticed that Gip seemed to have no use of his left side. Because his injury was on his brain's right side, which controls the body's left side, the concern was that Gip's left side might be damaged, perhaps even paralyzed.

So not every moment was a celebratory one. But that made us all the more determined to celebrate each blessing that we did have. No matter how small Gip's feats, we rejoiced. And we vowed not to let tomorrow's worries steal today's joys.

CHAPTER 9

Lives Left Behind

With the uncertainties surrounding Gip's condition, we had no way to know what we might be facing or how long we would be in Savannah. At best, we had a long journey ahead.

Even though it had only been a few days, our normal-life concerns were beginning to surface. Richard and I both had to address our job situations. It wasn't easy to answer the question of when we would return to work. Richard's boss, Dan, was very compassionate, telling him to take care of his family first. He kept Richard's projects moving forward and stayed on top of things during this uncertain time. My job was brand-new. I had been there for only one week when this accident happened, and it didn't appear I would be back anytime soon. I think we all knew that. But they were kind enough to tell me they'd hold onto my position "for as long as they could."

Taylor had just started his first year of high school, and we were concerned about his absence as well. Family and friends were already offering to take him home with them. They also offered to bring him back to Savannah on weekends or whenever we felt it necessary.

We had been greatly encouraged by the fact that Gip was slowly but surely waking from his coma, so we felt it best if we at least tried to put some normalcy back in Taylor's life. Sadly, we knew he would carry this burden with him no matter where he went, but it seemed to be the right decision to send him home with friends.

Unexpectedly, Taylor asked if he could stay with one of his *new* friends, David Isbill. We didn't know the Isbill family very well and reminded Taylor that he had offers to stay with friends whose families we were very close to. But Taylor looked at us with grown-up determination in his eyes and said, "I have prayed about this. Please let me go where God is leading me." He assured us that the Isbills were a good family and that they wanted him to stay with them.

We were so physically and emotionally exhausted at that time we could not make any sound decisions. Finally, Richard, Taylor, and I sat on the floor just outside Gip's room in the ICU and prayed together, pleading for divine discernment. Before I knew it, I was on the phone with David's mom, Jan. First words out of her mouth were "I know you don't know us that well, but I believe that God wants Taylor here. And I promise we'll do everything we can to help him through this." I was so overwhelmed by her kindness and her specific choice of words that I was already at ease about Taylor's choice to stay with this family.

Jan went on to say that she and her husband, Edward, had raised five children and David was the only one still at home. She said they had plenty of room in their house—and their hearts—for our child. We all agreed that this would be the right place for Taylor, and off he went.

Through God's grace, this loving family did have room for Taylor. They treated him as if he was one of their own. They fed and clothed him, took him to ball practices and games, laundered his clothes, helped him with his homework, picked up poster boards for his school projects, and so much more. As we spoke with Taylor each evening from Savannah, we were greatly comforted that he was not only well taken care of, but well loved.

Jan has since told us that prior to Gip's accident she felt as if God had been preparing her heart for an opportunity to help others. She had no idea what it might be, but when her son told her of Gip's accident and asked if Taylor could stay with them, she knew that was it. Right away she replied, "Yes!"

Since then, we have become like family to all the Isbills and will cherish their kindness and friendships forever. Taylor and David have remained close friends and even became college roommates. They also joined the same fraternity and are brothers in that way as well. How cool is that?

CHAPTER 10

Home Away From Home

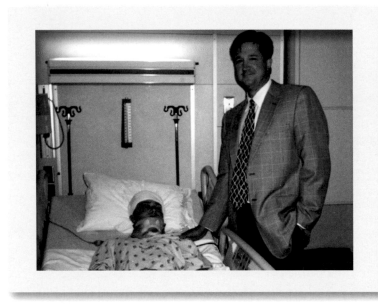

Gip with Dr. Louis Horn, the neurosurgeon who saved his life.

A fter a few days, thanks to the loving offers of many who donated their frequent-user hotel points, we were given a room at a local hotel. It was such a generous gift, and we were immensely grateful. The hotel was only minutes from the hospital, but we still fought leaving; we were anxious about being gone, even for a few hours.

Gip was still in ICU, though, and we were only allowed five-minute periods with him every other hour. There were no visiting hours during the night. So finally, after much coaxing from family and friends reminding us of the long road ahead, we acknowledged our need for rest, not to mention a shower. After receiving assurance from the medical staff that they'd contact us if Gip's condition changed, we loaded our belongings and headed out.

As soon as Richard and I walked into the hotel room, we closed the door behind us, sat on the edge of the bed together, and fell backward onto the mattress. From the very beginning, we had been surrounded by family and friends. We were and still are very thankful for all who came to be with us. But this was a private moment we had not yet had.

I'll never forget the look on my husband's face as we lay there, alone for the first time in days, finally able to let our guard down. It was just us—raw, transparent, and brokenhearted. He gently took me in his arms and held me as tightly as he could. I wrapped my arms around him with all the strength I had left. Facing each other but not saying a word, we lay there and wept, each engulfed in our own heartache. We awoke two hours later in the same position, holding on just as tightly as we had when we first embraced.

We got up, showered, and headed back to the hospital.

We spent every waking moment either in Gip's ICU cubicle or in the waiting area just outside it. We longed to be as close to him as we possibly could. When things were somewhat stable at night, we went to the hotel for a shower and a few hours' rest. We made arrangements with the neuro-surgeon and hospital staff to contact us if anything changed. Dr. Horn was kind enough to call every morning around six o'clock, after he made his early hospital rounds.

At night we set the alarm clock to be sure we were awake before Dr. Horn's call. Even though we were expecting it, our bodies jumped every morning when the phone rang. "Hello?" we answered with questioning voices. "Is he all right?" is what we really meant. Dr. Horn understood our anxiety and always got right to the point.

Profoundly exhausted, neither of us trusted ourselves to remember what the doctor told us, let alone be able to repeat it clearly to others. So when Dr. Horn called, we sat right next to each other on the bed with the phone carefully wedged between our ears and the speaker volume as loud as it would go. We rarely breathed during those calls fearing we might miss a word. We had a pad and pen next to the bed to write down everything the doctor said.

When Gip Gayle arrived via life flight at our trauma center, his condition was extremely critical. He had suffered a very severe brain injury, and we knew his survival was in question. He and his family have been through an ordeal that would test the faith of the best of us and that most will never experience. I have no doubt that the love of family and their faith in God was and is a critical part of Gip's recovery.

—Dr. Louis Horn, chief neurosurgeon of
Memorial University Medical Center, Savannah, Georgia

Dr. Horn carefully explained his concerns. He tried to give us good news whenever he could, but there was often bad news that followed; that's just how it was. His nature was amazingly calm, and we always felt great comfort to be in his care. We have no doubt that God planned for Dr. Horn to be on call that fateful day. Truly, he saved our son's life.

CHAPTER 11

From Friends to Family

Uncle Chuck

Because Gip was in such critical condition, the hospital would allow only family members in the ICU room. On day four, Gip's football coach and Young Life mentor, Chuck, came to Savannah. He brought along another of Gip's YL friends and mentors, Scott Spears. We knew how much their visit would mean to Gip, so we told the nurses that Chuck was Gip's uncle. When she opened the door to let him in, Scott slipped in too. It was the first of many hospital rules we would break! From then on, each time Chuck came, we referred to him as "Uncle Chuck," and Scott soon became Gip's long-lost "cousin."

Gip was unable to speak at that time, and his eyes were still swollen shut, but he seemed to recognize his friends' voices and responded to their kind words with a slight turn-up of the right corner of his lip. Chuck told Gip to fight hard or he would have to go back to his old football coaching techniques of "thigh masters" to get Gip up and running. We all noticed that Gip's shoulders shook a bit with laughter at Chuck's attempts at humor. It was wonderful to see flashbacks of earlier times when these two enjoyed football and fellowship—and fun.

Then Scott leaned over Gip's bed and whispered, "Hey, Gip, can you keep a secret?" It took a while, but Gip finally squeezed his hand. Scott said he just found out that his wife was pregnant with their first child. He said not to tell anyone because they hadn't even told their parents. Scott told Gip that if he worked really hard in his recovery, he might be able to convince his wife to name the baby "Gip." We could see Gip's stomach muscles move with laughter. I smiled as I told Scott we would hold him to that promise.

Just before they left, the nurse walked in to check Gip's vital signs. One test checked his eyes for reaction to light. She gently lifted his left eyelid. It was still severely swollen, but she carefully raised the drooping pocket of skin just enough for Gip to peek out. Because of his injuries' severity and the spray of birdshot around his eyes, Gip's vision remained in question.

Chuck leaned over the bed, placing himself directly in front of Gip's left eye, and said, "Hey, Gipper, can you see me?" We were on pins and needles as we anxiously waited for Gip's hand-squeeze response. It wasn't immediate, but Gip eventually managed to squeeze Chuck's hand with a "once for yes" reply. We all celebrated.

The nurse privately cautioned us not to put too much stock in Gip's response, as it may be that he sees just sparks of light or moving figures. Since he couldn't speak, he had only a yes-or-no way to communicate. His "yes squeeze" told us that he could see, but not *what* he could see. Nonetheless, we were ecstatic with the hope that Gip's vision was intact.

As Chuck and Scott began to say their good-byes, Gip squeezed Chuck's hand so hard it hurt. Chuck laughed and said, "Well, Gipper, you certainly haven't lost your famous strong grip!" We all smiled and thought Gip would let go at that point, but he didn't. He held on to Chuck's hand, squeezing it even tighter. It was evident it meant a lot to have Chuck and Scott there. He did not want them to leave.

Chuck leaned in toward the left side of Gip's head, and he and Scott both began praying out loud. It was clear Gip was lifted by their presence. Soon after, the nurses came in to tell us Gip needed to rest. But Chuck didn't have the heart to pull away from Gip's gripping hand. Once again, the nurse told Gip that his visitors needed to leave. Chuck turned his head for a moment to regain his composure. He was visibly shaken when Gip finally let go. It was difficult to say goodbye to Gip. Chuck choked up as he promised to come back soon.

Even though it was four-thirty in the morning when Chuck and Scott finally arrived back home, Chuck sent an updated email to Gip's prayer warriors. He was so fired up about Gip's emerging recovery that he couldn't sleep. He wanted to share the day's happenings with everyone. The excitement in Chuck's words as he described what that day meant to him was overwhelming. One by one, he listed the miracles that had already taken place and gave glory to God for His mighty works in Gip's survival.

Thumbs-Up

The following day, day five, Gip was able to add a thumbs-up to his response repertoire, and that was the beginning of a whole new light for our family. We used—and probably abused—this form of communication as we took turns asking Gip, "Do you love *me*?" When we got our desired thumbs-up confirmation of Gip's love, it was like winning the lottery.

We were so thrilled we just burst into song. Yes, we actually started singing! And with all the singers in my family, there was some major har-

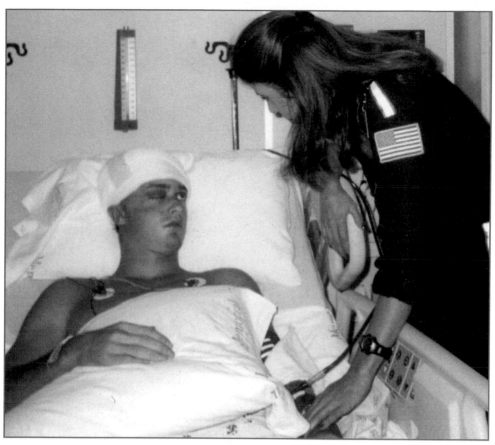

Gip with Alison Herrington, his life-flight nurse.

mony going on in that hospital. I'm sure many people thought we had lost our minds. Here we were in the Neuroscience ICU with one of the more critical patients they had probably seen in years, and we were singing. But miracles were happening right before our very eyes. We were singin' and celebratin'!

The doctors continued to test Gip's senses and reactions to stimuli. On the afternoon of day five, just as the nurse was about to lift Gip's eyelid and check his pupils and vision, in walked Gip's life-flight nurse, Alison.

Alison had been coming by every day to check on Gip. She was a part of this miracle and was determined to watch it unfold. With her kind heart and sweet nature, she quickly became like family to us. It touched our hearts the way she cared about Gip, about all of us.

As she stood at his bedside, the nurse lifted Gip's eyelid and asked if he could see his visitor. It was evident that he could see well enough to realize that his life-flight angel was quite an attractive young lady. As quickly as he could, he responded with a very enthusiastic thumbs-up.

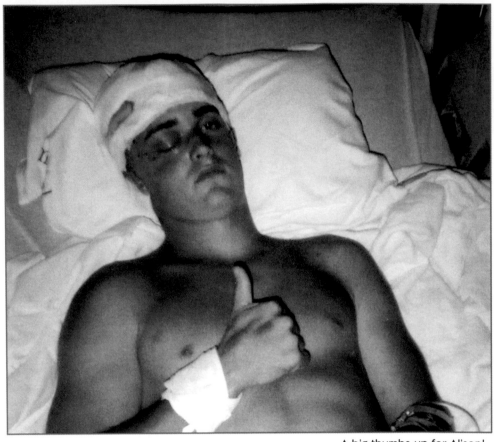

A big thumbs-up for Alison!

As soon as Alison left the room, Gip gave us his best smile possible and waved yet another emphatic thumbs-up.

His vision may not have been perfectly clear, but his approval sure was!

CHAPTER 12

It's a Miracle!

I Love You, Mom

As Gip showed improvement, the doctors began removing more and more tubes from his body. On day six, the nurses took out Gip's breathing tube. They rushed to the waiting room to tell us he was trying to speak.

We raced into his ICU room and surrounded his bedside with as much family as we could possibly fit in that little Number 10 cubicle. We greatly exceeded the number of visitors allowed, but we were so excited at the possibility of Gip talking that we all rushed in without permission. It happened so fast they didn't try to stop us. I do believe they were as thrilled as we were.

As we gathered around Gip's bedside, I leaned over and whispered in his ear, "It's Mom, Gip. Can you hear me?" We waited in complete silence as Gip struggled to move the words from his brain to his lips. He had intense concentration on his face as he worked hard to utter his first words. The doctors did not want him to strain, so the nurses kept telling Gip not to push himself too hard.

Much to my dismay, Gip's first words were *not* "I love you, Mom."

When Gip first came out of his coma, he could not see us, as his eyes were swollen shut. He was also unable to speak for a while because of the tubes in his mouth, so he could not ask questions. But he could hear us. We didn't realize that as Gip lay there listening to us tell him we were all at his side, it made him wonder who was at home taking care of his beloved dog, Yeller. So when they finally removed the tubes, Gip's first words were "How's Yeller?"

He was so weak and spoke so softly that we couldn't make out his exact words. But I was certain he was trying to say, "I love you, Mom." So I bent over the bed rail and leaned in close to his head as I whispered, "I love you, too, son."

Immediately we could see a bit of aggravation come over Gip's face. At first we thought it was because he was in pain. But then it became clear he was trying to speak again. I moved in even closer to hear what he was so desperately trying to tell us.

Then as clear as day he said, "Mom, I asked 'how's Yeller?'"

Everyone else was standing at the foot of Gip's bed anxiously waiting for me to repeat his dramatic first words. I'm sure I had a look of confusion—and disappointment!—on my face as I turned to them. I smiled and chuckled a bit as I said, "He asked 'how's Yeller?'"

We all roared with laughter. That was textbook Gip to be thinking about his dog above anything else! We assured him that Yeller was being well taken care of. As soon as he heard that, he began mustering the energy to say, "I love you, Mom," quickly followed by a "you too, Dad."

Once our family's laughter settled down, we suddenly realized that my dad was not in the room. Apparently he'd gone out for coffee when the nurses came to get us. We were so caught up in the moment that none of us noticed his absence. Richard ran to the coffee break-room, found my dad, and told him the great news. Together they rushed back to share in the joy. When we told Dad that Gip had asked about Yeller, he was visibly stunned. His body slumped over the bed rails.

You see, my dad is not just Gip's granddad—or "Pops," as he's fondly known to his sixteen grandchildren. He's also a physician, and he realized more than we did the magnitude of his grandson's first words. Dad had reviewed the CT scans. He'd seen medical evidence that Gip didn't have much chance to survive, let alone retain his memory or regain cognitive functions. He knew unmistakably that Gip needed nothing short of divine intervention. Well, we *had* divine intervention. In just one short week after being shot in the head, our son was talking!

With that, my dad leaned over and kissed Gip on the shoulder. He then looked back at us and said, "You do realize that we are witnessing a miracle,

As Gip's grandfather, receiving the call about his accident was devastating. As a physician, I knew the odds were not in his favor to survive, let alone recover. In Savannah, I looked at his CAT scans daily and knew of the damage and likely outcome. As time passed, it brought tears to my eyes as I realized that I was witnessing a miracle, we all were. It is truly remarkable that Gip's neuromuscular system functions entirely in normal fashion and that he can handle convoluted thought, including the most subtle humor, as well as he ever could—which exceeds the capacity of most of us. Without the grace of God, we would not be here today. I am a proud grandfather for the strength, courage, and faith Gip has shown through such adversity.

—Dr. Clifton Morris Jr., Gip's grandfather,
retired professor of radiology and pediatrics, LSU Medical Center,
and former chief of thoracic and cardiovascular radiology

don't you? This is nothing short of a miracle!" His voice got really loud when he said the word *miracle*.

We bowed our heads, and my dad led us in a prayer of thanks.

We couldn't wait to share this miraculous moment with Taylor. The second we left the ICU area, we called him. But Taylor wasn't home from football practice yet. Since I was about to pop to tell somebody, I blurted out our great news to Jan. She was in tears as she expressed her joy.

I asked her not to say anything to Taylor so that we could be the first to tell him. Of course I didn't have to actually ask for that courtesy; she knew. Jan was always careful not to discuss things with Taylor until after we had the chance to. Her awareness of and sensitivity to our needs—and Taylor's—was always right on target. We felt extremely blessed by the "mama" approach she took with every part of her caretaking.

Jan was always loving and tender with Taylor, never pushing him to talk but always there to listen in case he wanted to. She was thrilled that he would be receiving such glorious news that day.

When Taylor arrived at their home, Jan suggested that he give us a call to check on Gip before it got too late. He called right away.

"Mom, it's me. How's Gip?" he asked with hope in his voice.

I could hardly hold back the tears as I shouted out, "Oh, Taylor, he's talking. It's a miracle, son, a miracle! Gip is talking, and he remembers all of us."

"I knew he would, Mom, I just knew it!" he shouted back.

I wept as I told Taylor how proud I was of his powerful and positive spirit. I reminded him that God was answering our prayers. He agreed with great emphasis as he replied, "I never doubted it."

"I love you so much, son—so much!"

"I love you, too, Mom."

I handed the phone to Richard, and he and Taylor rejoiced at this amazing miracle.

Then Taylor asked, "So what did Gip say first?"

Of course Richard busted out laughing as he shared the funny story of Gip's first words. Taylor was quite amused as well and said, "That's Gip for ya!"

They wrapped up their call with the usual "I love you's" and "talk to you tomorrow's" and hung up. Taylor immediately shared the good news with his Isbill family.

We're on a Roll Now

By this time, Gip's miraculous recovery was drawing quite a bit of attention from all directions—family, friends, hospital staff, and other patients' families. Even the doctors were calling it a miracle. We were all amazed by Gip's progress.

On the morning of day seven, Gip was sitting up in bed. He struggled to stay balanced as his equilibrium remained unstable, and he continued to show no signs of feeling on his left side. But with his body propped with pillows for support, he was able to remain seated for nearly twenty minutes. Seeing him sitting up made him look healthier, which immeasurably lifted our spirits.

Then came another gift. The swelling around Gip's left eye was slowly subsiding. At lunchtime, his nurse suggested that he try opening his left eye. The doctors were still greatly concerned about damage to Gip's vision, so to truly test it the nurse did not tell Gip that Richard and I had entered the room. As he struggled to open his heavy lid, it suddenly popped open, and the nurse asked if he could see any light. Gip was able to speak, but it was still quite a challenge. Quietly, but with great affirmation, he replied, "I see more than light. I see my mom and dad." Richard and I rushed to his side and tearfully hugged him. What a gift it was to see that gorgeous green iris peeking out at us.

After that, every time we walked into Gip's ICU room, he looked at us through his one good eye and beamed his million-dollar half-smile. I've got a "mama-brag" moment here: Gip's high school classmates voted him as having the "Best Smile" as one of the Senior Superlatives noted in the yearbook. Oh, how we yearned to see that award-winning smile again.

At that time Gip was able to give only a partial smile because the smile muscles couldn't lift the left corner of his mouth. He had no feeling in that side of his face, but he smiled nonetheless, and we could just *feel* God's presence surround him.

By late afternoon on day seven, physical therapists were brought in to assess Gip's physical condition and needs. We watched in awe as they began working their magic. Within minutes they tested almost every muscle in his body. They also determined that Gip was, in fact, regaining feeling on his left side. It wasn't much, but it was enough for the doctors to express hope that his paralyzed state would not be permanent.

As the therapists continued to work with Gip, they gradually moved him to the bedside and with a tight grip on his entire body sat him straight up. Gip, being Gip, asked if they would let him walk. The therapists glanced at his doctor, who gave a nod of approval. What happened next stunned all of us, including Gip.

Two therapists lifted him off the bed and very carefully placed his feet upon the floor. They stood at his sides and grabbed his hips, chest, and shoulders to support him as the third therapist lifted Gip's legs, helping him

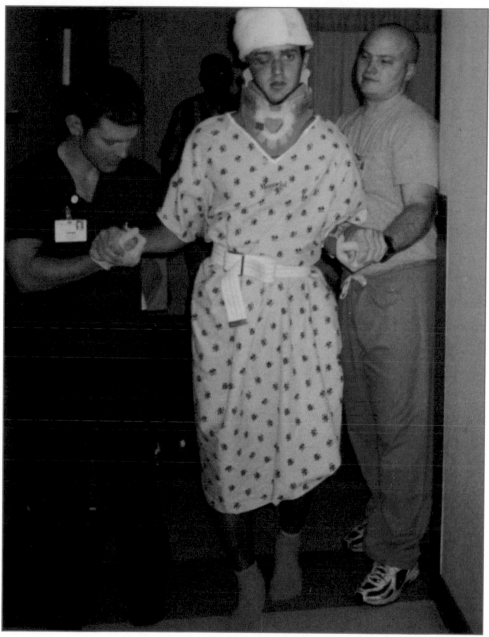

Gip taking his first real steps!

take three small steps. Despite the fact that his left side remained immobile, the therapists somehow managed to help him walk—three monumental steps toward hope, healing, and happiness. Gip's one good eye was glistening, his one mobile hand was waving a thumbs-up, and his perfect "half-smile" was lighting up the entire room. It was a glorious moment, providing evidence that Gip could recover.

CHAPTER 13

Power of Positive Thinking

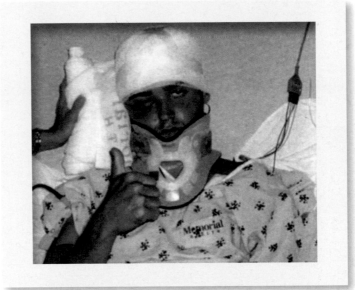

Gip showing determination with his thumbs-up attitude.

During the next few days, Gip continued to work hard and improved in every area. Speech therapists were brought in to work on his breathing, swallowing, and cognitive issues. He was learning how to swallow again, taking a few sips of water at a time, trying to build up to drinking a full glass of juice. Eating, however, was not as easy. We tried to spoon-feed him several soft foods, but he struggled to swallow and remained on an IV drip for his main source of fluids and nutrients.

His physical therapists continued to come by and work with him. He was very weak and unable to hold his body up by himself, but his therapists worked diligently to keep him progressing. With their strong arms and shoulders, they braced themselves on either side of our son as they gripped the harness wrapped around his waist. Carefully and slowly they helped him take a few steps each day. We could see Gip's athletic background kicking in as we watched him push through the pain, determined to keep on keepin' on.

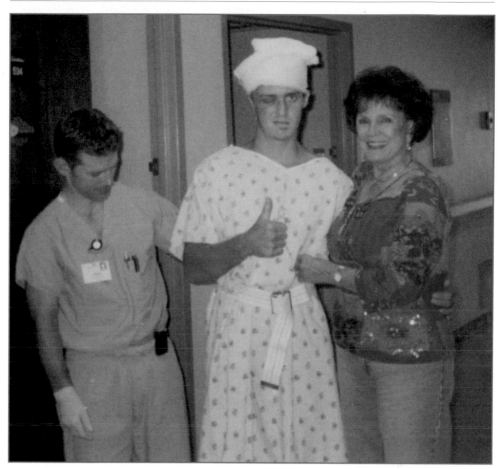

Gip walking with his grandmother, Honey.

Every twenty-four hours we noticed a gradual difference in Gip's left side; the feeling was returning slowly, but with certainty. They did extensive exercises to work out all his muscle groups, testing his other motor skills as well.

Gip's determination and positive attitude were already capturing the hearts of his caretakers. His unprecedented feats were being talked up by the entire medical staff, including the interns. When the surgeons made their rounds each day, they stopped by to show residents and interns their "miracle boy," as they called him. Most had thought Gip wouldn't be able to survive after suffering such a devastating brain injury, let alone show such remarkable and immediate signs of recovery.

On day ten, Gip was moved from the ICU into his own room. It was all happening so quickly, we were awestruck by his amazing recovery. Now that Gip was moved to a bed on the regular floor unit, we were allowed to be with him at all times. At first we were very excited about this, as we

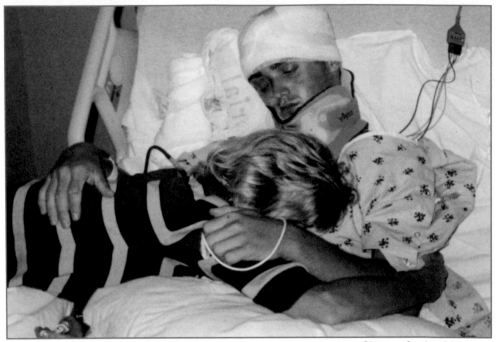

Gip comforting his mom.

had been limited to such short visits. But it was not the bed of roses we'd hoped for.

We didn't know how to handle the unexpected care that suddenly became our responsibility. Attendants handle everything for ICU patients. Once in their own room, however, they're closely monitored but not constantly cared for. Gip's medical needs were met, of course, but the rest was up to us.

Our son had suffered a traumatic brain injury; the hospital uses the term TBI. We became painfully aware what those three letters really meant. There are several stages of recovery from a brain injury. As wonderful as it was that Gip was becoming more mobile, that seemed to spark other issues. We soon realized that with a TBI, things can change quickly and without warning—and they did.

At this point, toward the second week's end, the numbness from Gip's injuries was beginning to wear off, and he started having severe headaches. The pain was excruciating at times, and often there was little they could do about it. Because Gip's injury was brain-related, there were some pain medications he was not allowed to take.

Gip had become extremely restless and required some real manhandling to restrain him at times. It was frightening to watch such bizarre behavior after things had been so calm. One minute he seemed fine, and

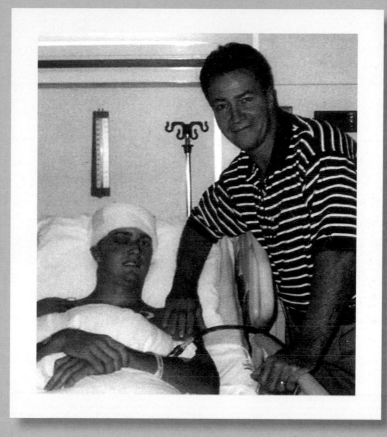

Gip with his dad.

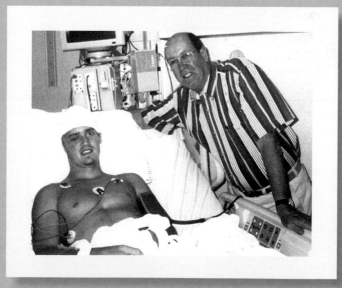

Gip with Uncle Paul, enjoying a good joke.

then the next he was almost out of control, trying to leave the bed, yanking out tubes and monitors. Watching our child suffer like that was unbearable. Many times I had to leave the room; it was just too difficult to witness his pain.

Richard stayed with Gip at night and practically forced me to go to the hotel for some much-needed rest. My mom and her brother, my Uncle Paul, were with me most of the time, and they practically had to drag me away. As tough as it was to see Gip in pain, I still couldn't bear to leave his side.

Several days later, Gip began to settle down and seemed almost stable. At that point I insisted that Richard and I take turns staying the night. My very first night on duty, things were going well. Gip was feeling pretty perky that day. He and I were even enjoying a few laughs as we watched a comedian on television. As we both got ready to go to sleep, we held hands and prayed together. Not long after, he dozed off.

Two hours later I was awakened by Gip's screams. His temperature had soared to an alarming 105 degrees. He was not only screaming but hallucinating. His body flopped aimlessly about his bed. Nurses came rushing in, and the next thing I knew, the surgeon was at his side and they were forcing me out of the room.

I called Richard but couldn't reach him. He was in the shower. My mom was in the hotel room next door to him, so I called her. She ran to Richard's room and banged on the door. Within minutes they were back at the hospital.

Gip had a major infection in his body, and it had caused his temperature to rise and his body to go into shock. His wound reopened, and he was facing yet another grueling surgery to repair it. His life was in danger again. It seemed we were back to square one in many ways.

After they rolled our son into surgery, we sat in the waiting room in total disbelief, barely able to whisper our cries to God. By this time it had been a couple of weeks since Gip's accident, and he'd overcome so much, so fast. We were all encouraged by his fast-paced recovery. But this setback had us feeling that his progress had been all for naught.

They were able to repair the wound, but it was still a very fragile area, and the doctors were concerned about the massive size of the opening and the lack of elasticity in the skin to keep it covered. We were thankful for the successful surgery but cautious about the impending complications.

The doctors warned us that Gip would need quite a bit of time to recover. And he did. He didn't just bounce back. He faced daily disappointments, and it was tough not to get discouraged. But Gip was determined to get

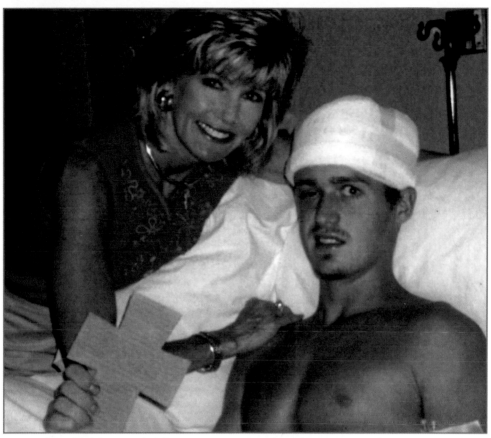

Gip with his mom, holding a cross engraved with the poem "Footprints in the Sand."

back to his therapies, and that made him push through the pain and sadness of this setback.

Our lack of sleep was beginning to take its toll, and we were all running out of steam. The days were long, the nights even longer. We knew the only way we were going to get through these trials was to dig deep and "walk by faith, not by sight." We had to overlook the earthly signals staring us in the face and somehow focus our hearts on placing our child completely in God's hands. We had to trust.

There is a lot to be said about the power of positive thinking. For us, that positive power comes from prayer. So pray we did. Sometimes we were holding on by a thread, but we were holding on, nonetheless. Together we prayed Gip's favorite Bible verse over and over again: *"I can do all things through Christ who strengthens me"* (Philippians 4:13).

We held on to every word of that verse as if our lives depended on it. Because they did!

CHAPTER 14

Filling the Gap

Our Football Lives

We missed Taylor's first high school football game, played two weeks after the accident. It was discouraging not to be part of such a special moment in his life. But we were well represented. Taylor had a huge cheerleading squad of family friends who helped carry him and his freshman team to victory.

Our friend Beverly put together a "bucket fund-raiser" for Gip. She called it "One for the Gipper." She and many helpers pasted Gip's high school football photo on water buckets that were passed around the stadium by the football players and cheerleaders during halftime of the season-opening games. There was also a "One for the Gipper" button campaign started by Gip's friend Ashley in which people donated funds in return for homemade buttons they wore to the game. In addition, our friends Jill and Laura created prayer ribbon pins for all to wear as a reminder to pray for our child. They painted Gip's name on one side and a cross on the other.

At halftime, for both the freshman team on Thursday night and the varsity team on Friday night, Collins Hill High School had a special game dedication for Gip where one of the football moms talked about his accident and the bucket fund-raiser. She asked for a moment of silence for Gip so that those present could offer their individual prayers. After the silence, the crowd broke into cheers. Prayers lifted up at a public high school football game—imagine that!

We heard so many wonderful stories about this dedication, we felt as if we were actually there. Chuck went to the Thursday-night game to cheer Taylor on. He brought a video camera and filmed all of Taylor's great plays. He also filmed several friends and coaches sending well wishes to Gip. The next day, Chuck came to Savannah to show Gip, Richard, and me how well Taylor played. It was awesome to see the game, even if it was after the fact. It helped us feel that we weren't *completely* missing out on Taylor's life.

That Friday afternoon after Taylor got home—his Isbill home—we called and congratulated him on his amazing game. As we spoke, I just purred

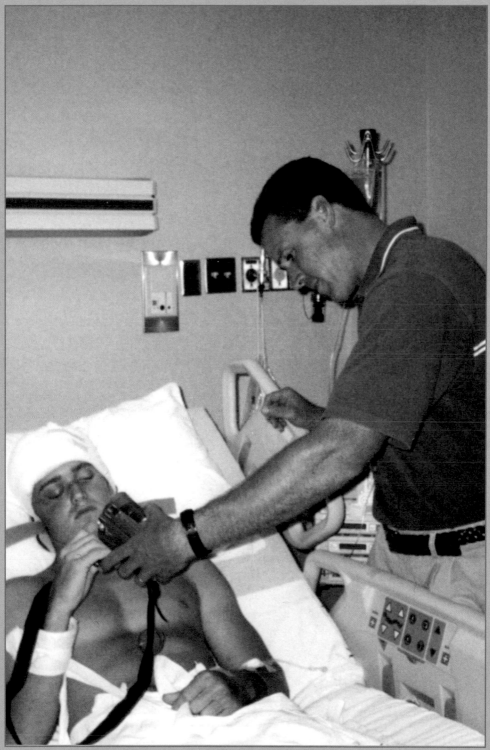

Coach Chuck showing Gip a video of Taylor's first high school football game.

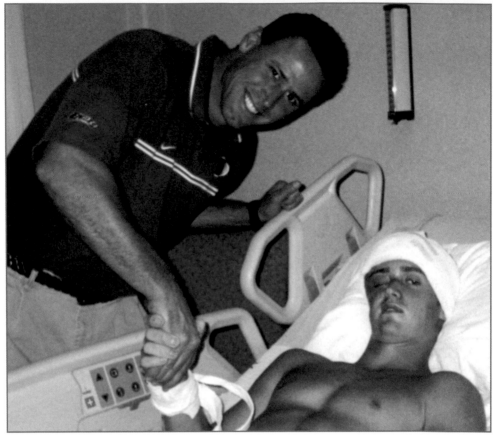

Gip thanking Coach Chuck for filming Taylor's game and coming all the way to Savannah to share it with us.

listening to the excitement in his voice. It was such a gift to know that Taylor was able to have some sense of normalcy in his life. I then handed the phone to Gip, and he talked with Taylor for a few minutes and told him how proud he was of him. Richard finished the call as Taylor gave him a blow-by-blow description of every play. As I watched Richard on the phone talking football with Taylor, I glimpsed our old lives peeking through: our boys playing ball and Richard beaming with pride as he coached and encouraged them. It was uplifting! I felt our lives were still intact, if only for a moment.

Keeping Vigil

Unfortunately, Gip's wound continued to open, causing doctors to keep him in a bit of a quarantine setting. To limit his exposure to germs, they allowed no visitors other than immediate family. Friends knew this, but it didn't stop them from making the long drive or flight to Savannah to be by our side. We would chat with friends in the waiting area and then go to Gip's room to tell him who came to visit. Soon we noticed that family and friends were taking shifts to be with us: they were keeping a vigil. When one earthly angel left, another one appeared.

One of Gip's oldest and dearest friends, Nick Disney, came to the hospital several times. When we told Gip that Nick was there, Gip said, "Tell Nick to tell his mom that she owes me a snowball fight!" This had been an ongoing joke between Gip and Nick's mom since Gip was eight years old. His memory of this joke was a huge gift to us at that time, because Gip had been showing signs of childhood memory loss.

For the first few days after Gip woke from his coma, it appeared his long-term memory was intact. But after a while, he began revealing large memory gaps, and we were greatly concerned. Realizing that Gip not only remembered who Nick was, but recalled something from their childhood ten years earlier, gave us hope that Gip's long-term memory was returning. We ran to the waiting room and shared his snowball fight comment with Nick, and we all had a great laugh about the Gipper still being the Gipper.

On weekends, friends drove Taylor to Savannah. They also brought several of his friends with them. It was very moving to Richard and me to see these fine young men gather around Taylor in *his* time of need. Of course it was a blessing for us to see our precious child again. I do believe I hugged Taylor tighter than I ever had before. But he didn't seem to mind; he knew how much we missed him. He knew we needed to hold him in our arms and love on him for as long as he was there. We ached when he left, but our pain was greatly eased as we witnessed the wonderful support system he had. Those young men—and their parents—truly rallied around Taylor, and we will always love them for that.

Slowly but surely, after a couple of weeks, Gip started to show signs of progress again. We were elated at the pendulum swinging back in his favor. It was a struggle, but he finally began sitting up again, with assistance. He was relearning how to eat and drink. And amazingly, not long afterward Gip was walking again, with the help of a walker and several therapists at his side. He was still very weak, but other parts of his recovery were gradually improving, and we were thankful for this new hope on the horizon.

About four weeks into his recovery, Gip started showing signs of short-term memory loss. His long-term memory seemed to have returned, and we celebrated that gift many times. But we had not given much thought to his short-term memory, until signs of forgetfulness began to emerge. It became most apparent after my mom left Savannah and Gip repeatedly asked for her even though we had already explained her absence.

As much as it pained her to leave, she had to return to Louisiana for *her* medical care. Just months before Gip's accident, Mom had finished chemotherapy treatments for colon cancer. Of course she and Dad dropped everything and came to Savannah as soon as they got the call about Gip. But after a few weeks, it was imperative that she go home for her cancer follow-up appointments. It was very emotional for my mom; she couldn't bear to leave Gip's side. I do believe her heart ached as much as mine. Finally, Dad and my brothers convinced her to take care of herself, promising that she could return in a few days.

Even in that short period, we missed my mom immensely. We certainly wanted her to take care of herself, but we anxiously awaited her return. Mom's the kind of person who lights up a room when she enters. Anybody who knows her will tell you the same. "Honey" is her grandmother name, and she is just that—she's everybody's Honey.

Gip had become quite dependent on my mom, and so had we; selfishly, we hated to see her leave. She was away only for a few days, but it was quite a reunion when she returned, as we all basked in Honey's "light."

Fortunately, when one family member would leave, another came as a replacement. Quite often when there was a break in the vigil, my Uncle Paul drove in from North Carolina at a moment's notice, making certain we were never left alone.

Gip is a huge Uncle Paul fan, so having him around helped keep things upbeat and humorous, as he always had a good joke to share. In addition to bringing much-needed laughter, Uncle Paul provided an endearing listening ear for me and a strong shoulder for Richard to lean on.

Want to Take a Vacation?

As weeks passed, we spent hour upon hour in the hospital waiting room. When things were stable with Gip, we went to our hotel for a few hours of late-night rest. Living out of suitcases between the hospital and the hotel, we were growing wearier by the day. We had not been home in more than a month. Our older son, just a few feet down the hall, was fighting for his life. Our younger son was back home, almost five hours away, trying to resume *his* broken life without us there to help him.

We were also quite concerned about what would happen to our jobs after being gone for so long ... and possibly longer. At that point, we both still had our positions, but time was dragging out, and so were our worries.

Even little things added to the strain, like the fact that a television in the waiting room was always on. Sometimes that made us crazy when we wanted peace and quiet. But there were other families there, and the television was left on for them. Most of the time, we tried to ignore it and focus on rest and prayers. But lacking other diversions, many times we ended up watching whatever was on.

One evening we found ourselves watching a television show about world travel. It was showcasing vacation hot spots from Hawaiian beaches to the Swiss mountains.

As we watched, I was resting my head on Richard's shoulder. After a few minutes, I turned and whispered in his ear, "Let's pretend we are on vacation somewhere. If you could pick any place in the whole world to go, where would you want to take our family right now?"

Without hesitating, Richard turned his head toward me, gently lifted my chin, and said "Home—I'd want to take my family *home.*"

That pretty much said it all. Home sweet home is the best place in the world, especially when you're hurting. We yearned to have our little family home—safe and sound, everyone neatly tucked in their beds, all four present and accounted for—like it's supposed to be.

CHAPTER 15

Careful What You Ask For

With a brain injury, immediate and aggressive therapy makes a huge difference in the long-term outcome. So after nearly five weeks of level one trauma care in Savannah, Gip's doctors discharged him to begin treatment at Shepherd Center, a world-renowned rehabilitation facility in Atlanta, Georgia. This center is approximately forty-five minutes from our home. After being away for so long, we were ecstatic to be back with our son Taylor, our dog Yeller, and our wonderful support group of family and friends.

But Gip was in severe pain the day the ambulance came to transport him to Atlanta, and we were all concerned how he would handle the long drive. When the emergency vehicle arrived, I told the medics about Gip's condition and asked if I could ride with them so that I could comfort my child during the trip. The driver said they don't normally allow it, but he would agree to it that time since Gip was in such obvious distress. I was so thankful that I gave the man a great big hug.

Once they had Gip situated on the gurney and lifted into the ambulance, I proceeded to climb in behind him. But the driver took my arm and escorted me to the front of the ambulance, explaining that his offer was for me to ride in the front of the vehicle, not the back.

I told him I didn't understand, that I'd seen many family members in the back of an ambulance with loved ones and I wanted the same courtesy. Well, according to the driver and unlike what we've all seen in movies and on TV, the law allows only the patient and the EMT in the back of an emergency unit.

Disgruntled, I sat in the front passenger seat across from the driver. I had to turn my head completely around the whole time just to get a glimpse of my son in the back of the wagon.

It was a long and bumpy six-hour ride from Savannah to Atlanta, and Gip was in utter agony the whole time. His pain elevated with each passing hour, and he began crying out every time we hit a bump in the road—and we hit many. As he lay there begging me to help him, I begged the driver to stop for a minute and let me console him. I even tried to unbuckle my seatbelt and go to his aid. But the driver threw his arm across my seat, informing me in no uncertain terms that I was not allowed in the back.

After several hours of relentless pain, Gip began throwing up. The EMT handed him a bucket but offered no other source of comfort. He kept telling me that Gip's vitals were being monitored and that I had nothing to be concerned about.

"Concerned? Are you kidding?" I replied. "That is my child back there, and he is in unbearable pain. I am way past *concerned,* mister. Why can't I just go to him for a few minutes to comfort him?"

Without so much as glancing in my direction, both the driver and the EMT told me I needed to remain seated until we were in the Shepherd Center parking lot. By this time I was a basket case, sorry I had ever asked to ride in the ambulance. My hope had been to sit next to my child and comfort him during the transport. But instead I was forced to watch him suffer for six long hours with no way to ease his pain.

I understand that there are safety regulations. I am thankful for such things. And I certainly wanted them to focus on driving with care and caution. I have always honored and respected the positions of such public servants, realizing the difficulties and dangers they face in their jobs. But it seemed that the human factor of compassion was missing. With my child in so much pain, I just wanted a few minutes to safely pull over to the side of the road so I could calm him.

Richard was following the ambulance in our car, packed with belongings from our month-and-a half stay in Savannah. As Gip continued to cry out for help, I called Richard and told him how much pain Gip was in and that the driver would not let me comfort him. Of course the driver heard my conversation, as we were both seated in the front of the ambulance. I wanted him to hear me! Richard asked to speak with the driver, but the driver refused to take the phone, stating that it was a safety violation for him to talk on the phone while operating an emergency vehicle.

Afraid my actions might cause more problems for Gip, I finally stopped fighting. I didn't want the driver distracted. After all, he was carrying precious cargo. So I sat there in my buckled-up prison chair and listened to my child suffer. But each time Gip cried out for help, I glanced at the driver. Okay, I *glared* at him!

Shouting just to be heard over the grinding engine noises, I kept telling Gip how well he was doing and reassured him that we were almost there. Six hours of "almost there" just about took the life out of both of us. I tried to comfort Gip by reminding him that his dad was right behind us. I told him to look out the little hole in the back window where he could see his dad waving to him. Richard waved to Gip frequently during the six-hour drive. Gip tried to wave back but was getting weaker by the minute.

When we finally reached Shepherd Center, I quickly unbuckled, jumped out of my seat, ran to the back of the ambulance, and held my precious, hurting child in my arms. He was so weak, he could barely breathe. When he saw my face, he looked up and asked, "Are we there yet, Mom?"

I broke down in tears as I whispered, "Yes, son, we're here. We're finally here."

CHAPTER 16

Relearning Life

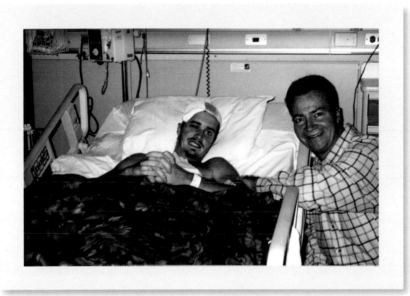

Gip enjoying a laugh with his dad.

Shepherd Center Rehab

Ah, Shepherd Center! I simply cannot sing its praises enough. From the moment we walked into this world-renowned rehabilitation center, we could practically smell recovery in the air.

Hope is what Shepherd is all about; it's built into virtually everything that happens at the center. By this time, Gip was going into his recovery's sixth week, and we were all banking on that "Shepherd hope."

Dr. Donald Leslie, Shepherd Center's medical director, met us at the door as we walked in. His kind, professional manner set the tone right away, making us feel welcome and secure. After he introduced himself, I looked at him with desperation pouring out of me and tearfully whispered, "Please help us."

He gently took my hand and said, "It's going to be a tough journey. But I promise we'll do everything we can to help make your son whole again." Hope. That's what we wanted to hear, and that's what we held on to for dear life. Dr. Leslie quickly became like family to us.

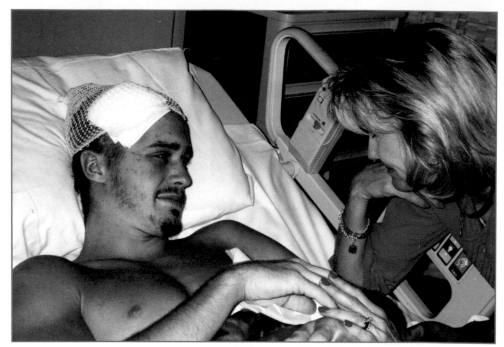

Gip sharing a tender moment with his mom.

Everyone could see the distress we were in from our unnerving ambulance ride. They took us directly up to Gip's room and helped him get settled in. He was clearly exhausted from the trip. They gave him some pain medication, and he finally fell asleep.

While Richard was unpacking Gip's belongings, I pulled up a chair and pushed it next to Gip's bed as close as I possibly could. I stuck my arm through the side rails and gently put my hand over his while he rested. Tears streamed down my cheeks as I thanked God for bringing us to safety at Shepherd Center. As uncomfortable as it was, I rested my head on the cold metal rails between us and began drifting off to sleep myself.

Several hours later, Gip's therapy staff came to his room and introduced themselves. It was evident from the start that these were well-trained professionals. They immediately did a comprehensive evaluation and began developing Gip's customized rehabilitation program. Within an hour, Gip and his therapy team were swapping humorous one-liners.

As time went on, humor became the common bond that helped carry Gip through eight long hours of therapy each day. The grueling tasks of Shepherd Center's intense programs proved to be quite a challenge for him.

But that's what was necessary to recover, and that's what makes Shepherd so successful. The crowning glory of it all was the aggressive but gentle way his therapists poured their hearts and souls into helping Gip recover.

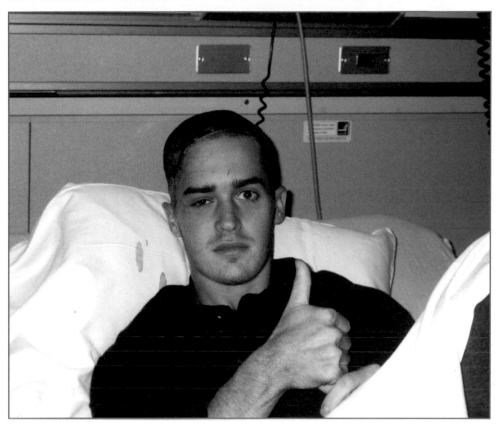

Gip unveiled!

Between Margaret Sharp, his physical therapist, Kathy Farris, his occupational therapist, Jennifer Douglas, his speech therapist, Ashley Haynes, his recreational therapist, and Brandi Bradford, his therapist technician, Gip was well cared for. It wasn't long before we realized they would soon be our new best friends.

With each passing day, we noticed the immense compassion of Gip's therapists and felt certain that God had divinely selected each one for our child—and for our family. As we watched them carefully and tenderly encourage Gip through every challenge, we witnessed their character, integrity, enthusiasm, and genuine desire to see our child succeed. This was clearly much more than just a job for them; it was a God-driven purpose.

Due to the nature of some brain injuries, Shepherd Center employs behavioral technicians. Most of the time, they help with physical therapies and motor-skill exercises. But sometimes their job includes assisting patients who are easily confused or unaware of their surroundings, trying such things as escaping their wheelchairs or leaving a room unattended. We were fortunate Gip didn't require that kind of therapy. But he did benefit from their

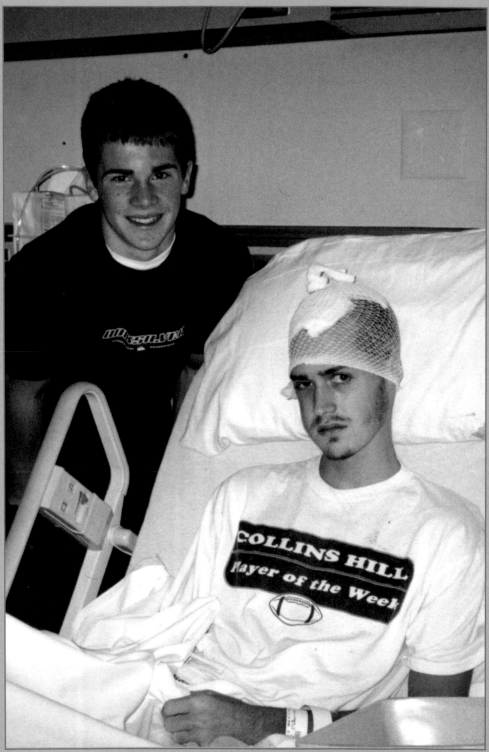

Gip working hard to deal with pain while trying to enjoy Taylor's weekend visits.

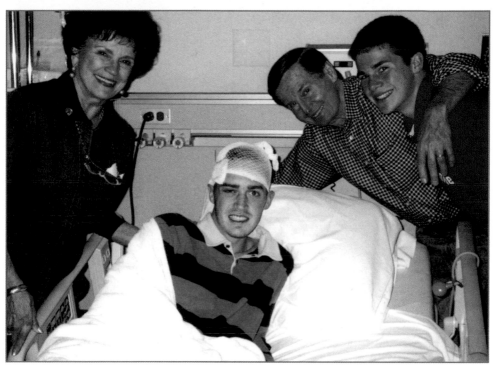

Gip enjoying a visit with Honey, Pops, and Taylor.

strong physical support, as he often tried to master challenges before he was able. They were always there to support him, making certain he never fell or hurt himself.

Gip thoroughly enjoyed being around these guys, as they entertained everyone with their silly antics. One behavioral technician in particular, Sean Burage, really reached out to Gip, going way beyond the call of duty. During Gip's toughest times, when he was unable to get out of bed and had to lie still for days on end, Sean would bring a deck of cards and entertain Gip with magic tricks. Talk about a heart of gold. This man had a wife and several kids at home, but he still made time after his busy work day to walk down to Gip's room to bring joy and laughter, where there had been none all day.

To help the patient and the family deal with such a life-changing event, Shepherd Center provided us with volumes of reading material about traumatic brain injuries. We learned that a TBI is like no other injury. Shepherd not only put us through several TBI education classes and family training sessions but also provided information about support groups of all kinds to help families deal with this level of trauma. All this was very helpful, as most of us were rather lost in our new roles as TBI caretakers. But as much as we needed this information, it was still hard to digest it, realizing how many struggles lay ahead for our child, for all of us.

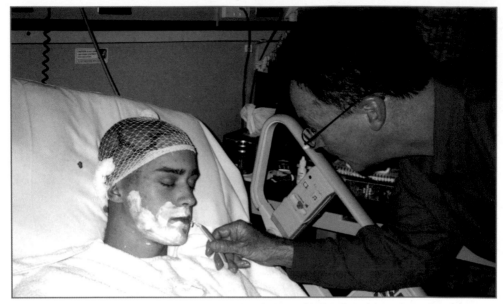

Richard giving Gip his first shave since the accident.

Some days I wanted to bury my head in the sand and pretend that every-thing was just fine. But there was simply no getting around the grim reality. Things were not fine, and we had a long road ahead.

Gip was now living at Shepherd Center; he was completely in its care. He had to basically start over with *everything,* not just remaster his physical deficits. He had to relearn how to do the simplest of tasks. They call this ADL (activities of daily living). Even though he was well into in his second month of recovery, Gip still had to be retaught how to properly swallow, eat, and talk. He had to work on sitting up, leaning, and standing. And, of course, he continued to work on walking skills and stability. These were all major challenges. He even had to relearn how to hold a spoon and fork, how to brush his teeth, how to take a shower, how to shave, how to get dressed— and that's just the short list.

These weren't just physical challenges for Gip; they were mental chal-lenges as well. Often he would get in the shower and just sit there, unable to remember how to turn on the water or what to do with the soap and washcloth. Many times Gip's showers took more than an hour to complete. The therapists advised us not to intervene because Gip needed to learn these things himself. There were times he couldn't remember how to button a shirt or tie his shoelaces. They helped him along to a point, but then he had to work on his memory skills to complete the task.

Dinner time was just as frustrating for Gip. Even though he was hungry and wanted to eat, he would often just sit at the table staring at his food.

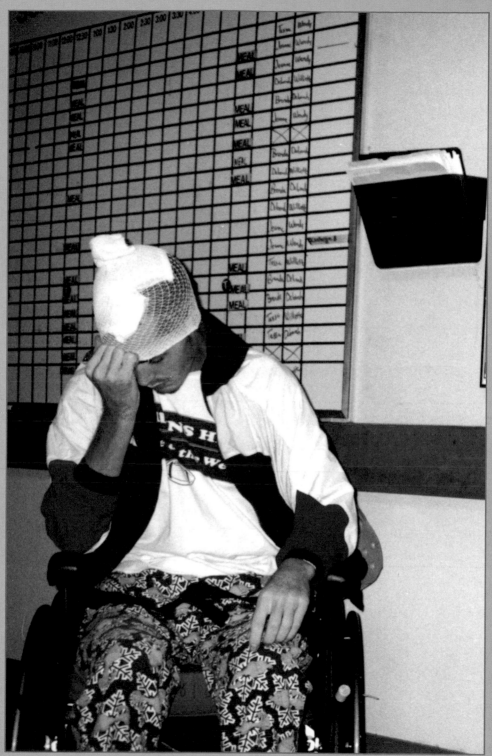

Gip struggling to get through the day.

Gip working hard to catch a ball during a physical therapy exercise.

He knew the food was there for him, but he couldn't figure out how to pick up his fork and get the meat off his plate and into his mouth. Sometimes, something as simple as eating a sandwich took hours out of his day.

It was difficult for Gip to think clearly at first. He couldn't remember things in order. His thoughts seemed to be "all jumbled up," as he would say. Some days he would wake up and get dressed, only to turn around minutes later and begin getting ready for bed, as if the day were over. He had to have constant direction on what was going on and what he needed to do next. He also struggled with remembering things by rote in proper order or sequence. Counting items was quite a challenge. Following even the simplest of commands took huge amounts of concentration and time. He sometimes became so exhausted from the mental workout that he fell asleep in the middle of a task.

Relearning how to read and write, and then to comprehend it all, was a slow process as well. Gip's short-term memory loss made it extremely difficult for him to remember what he had just relearned. It broke our hearts to watch him work so hard on something, only for him to forget it the next day and have to start all over. His deficits ran across the board, affecting every aspect of his life. Even such things as working a television

Gip walking the hallways with an IV and therapists at his side.

remote control, a CD player, or a cell phone had to be retaught. *Nothing* came easily.

As parents, we wrestled with our new roles as well, never certain when we should step in or step out. Having the knee-jerk reaction of wanting to do things for Gip, we soon learned we were not helping but hindering his recovery. It was heartbreaking to watch our son struggle. As tough as it was to watch, we knew we had to let Gip do things on his own, no matter how difficult it was or how long it took to accomplish each task.

There were many therapy sessions in which family was not to be involved, so as not to disrupt the patient's concentration. Other than those times, I

Gip with family, getting ready for a walk around the hallway.

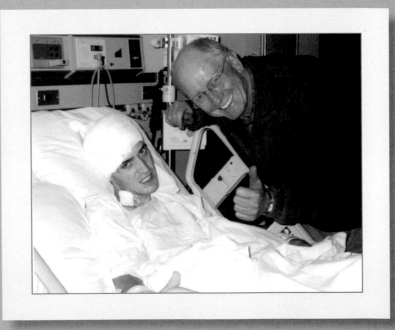

Gip with Uncle Ed. With continuous infections, Gip's weight
sometimes fluctuated dramatically. There were times when his
weight dropped to scarcely more than 100 lbs.

never left Gip's side. We were there to cheer him on for every attempt and every accomplishment, no matter how small. We were also there to console him on the tasks he could not complete, and there were many.

We did our best to stay focused on celebrating every good moment we had. With Gip's amazing doctors and therapists at his side—and ours—we felt the hope we so desperately needed. It was clear by their actions and gentleness that they were there to help our entire family get our lives back.

Isolation

Now that we were at Shepherd Center and much closer to home, many of Gip's friends, and ours, drove to Atlanta's Buckhead area to visit. They couldn't wait to see Gip. We were very touched by the attention, but they didn't realize that Gip was still in a very critical situation.

How could they know? Word on the street was that Gip was out of a coma, he was talking, his memory was back, and he was even beginning to walk again. For all intents and purposes, he was healed and well on his way to a full recovery.

Everybody was in awe of Gip's miraculous recovery, and so were we. It *was* miraculous how far Gip had come. Just six weeks earlier, he had been shot in the head—in the *head!* By all medical accounts, Gip wasn't supposed to survive, let alone be talking and walking.

But as glorious as it all was, Gip was still unable to have visitors. Despite several surgeries, his wound remained open, putting him at a very high risk for infection. Just being in a hospital environment presented an enormous level of exposure to germs. The doctors advised us to keep visitors to a minimum since each person that came in contact could pose further risks.

Having always enjoyed the fun and laughter of being with family and friends, we discovered this newfound isolation to be quite a challenge. But we had to protect Gip however we could. So not only was he unable to have visitors, we were unable to have visitors as well.

"Uncle Chuck" was pretty much the only exception. But one of my dear friends, Jill, just happened to work at Piedmont Hospital, which is next door to Shepherd Center, connected by a tunnel. It was a gift beyond gifts. Chuck and Jill were our only contacts with the outside world. They checked on Gip and me several times a week, bringing us non-hospital meals, special orthopedic pillows for my aching neck, and humorous little gifts for Gip, in hopes of bringing a smile to his face during those painful times. They were the only ones who saw what we were really facing, and it was comforting to have them around to talk about it. It would have been difficult to make it without them by our side.

More often than not, however, I sat by myself. The silence was deafening at times. Gip spent eight grueling hours a day in therapy and took long naps each afternoon from sheer exhaustion. We muddled through one day to the next with uncertainty lurking around every corner. Some days Gip's recovery was moving along amazingly well, but other days his body would shut down, going into distress from high fevers and infections.

There were several times during the next few months when things became extremely critical for Gip—and overwhelming for us. Quite often these issues happened during the day when Richard was at work, almost two hours away, and I was facing these crises alone. Handling that level of fear was a challenge. With all the ups and downs, we never knew from day to day what the outcome of all this would be.

I remember one time in particular when Gip was taking a nap. He had been having a fairly stable day, so I felt comfortable stepping out of his room for a little while. I quietly made my exit and headed to the hospital garden area for a change of scenery and a little fresh air. I was gone only about fifteen minutes. As I was returning, I could see Gip's doorway jammed with doctors, nurses, and medical equipment. I panicked as I heard them screaming "STAT! STAT!" When they saw me come flying around the corner, the doctor turned to the nurses and shouted, "Get the mother out of here!"

Situations like that occurred more times than I can bear to recall. It's hard to explain each crisis in detail—what happened, why it happened, what they did to combat it, and how many surgeries it led to. Bottom line: there were a *lot* of uncertainties inherent in Gip's condition, and he faced one complication after another because of them.

Many friends stopped by to take me to lunch or get me out of the hospital setting for a short while. They were hoping to whisk me away from it all, if only for a moment, to give me a much-needed break. But with all the behind-the-scenes scares and the close calls we continued to experience, I was simply too frightened to leave Gip's side.

During those times of isolation, Gip and I often reminisced about the "good ol' days." We talked about the great times our family had together— camping in the mountains, trips to the beach, snow skiing in Colorado—and the fun we had during their Little League years while Richard coached the boys and I handled "team mom" duties of snacks, trophies, and team parties. We laughed many times as we shared memories of Louisiana holidays with our huge extended family and the crazy antics that took place when we all got together. Humor has always been a big part of our family's enjoyment of life, and remembering those good times made us more determined to fight hard, to get back to the life we once had.

When Gip was sleeping and I wasn't drifting down memory lane or napping, I went straight to prayer. I did this to remind myself that I was never truly alone, that God was always close at hand, at heart. With my eyes shut tightly, I envisioned Him wrapping His arms around me. As silly as it may sound, I always imagined Jesus on my right side. So whenever I was in need of His light, I looked to my right, and there He was.

Happy Birthday, Dad!

Gip was making great progress in his rehab at Shepherd Center, but unfortunately his wound continued to open. Severe infections resulted, which led to even more surgeries. One surgery happened to fall on Richard's birthday. I don't think any of us had a clue what day or even what month it was. We had long since lost all sense of time and order. We certainly weren't thinking about birthdays. It was all we could do just to get through each day, let alone be aware of special calendar events.

But once again, Gip amazed us with his cognizance. When he woke up in the recovery room, he asked for Dr. Leslie. As soon as Dr. Leslie walked into the ICU, Gip asked if he could borrow some money. Unable to imagine anything Gip would need money for at such a time, Dr. Leslie assured him that whatever he might need, they could get for him. But Gip continued to press, asking only for a few dollars and promising to pay it back as soon as he got out of the hospital.

At this point, Dr. Leslie assumed Gip must still be a bit out of it from the anesthesia's effects, so he agreed to give Gip whatever money he needed. Gip thanked him, explained that it was his dad's birthday, and said he just needed enough money to get a birthday card and a balloon.

This brought tears to Dr. Leslie's eyes, along with everyone else in the ICU who heard it. A young man fighting for his life had just undergone major brain surgery and was not fully cognizant, but he remembered his dad's birthday and was worried he didn't have a gift. Dr. Leslie said he would be honored to get these gifts for Richard.

Right away, he went down to the hospital gift shop and bought a card and balloon. He came back to the ICU, held Gip's arm steady so he could sign the card for his dad, and then tied the balloon to Gip's bedside table. Gip thanked Dr. Leslie and immediately dozed off, able to rest peacefully knowing his dad's birthday would be properly celebrated. As Dr. Leslie left the room, he called the cafeteria staff and asked them to make a birthday cake for Richard.

Hours later, the room was filled with hospital staff anxiously awaiting Richard's arrival. The moment he walked in, Richard was greeted with

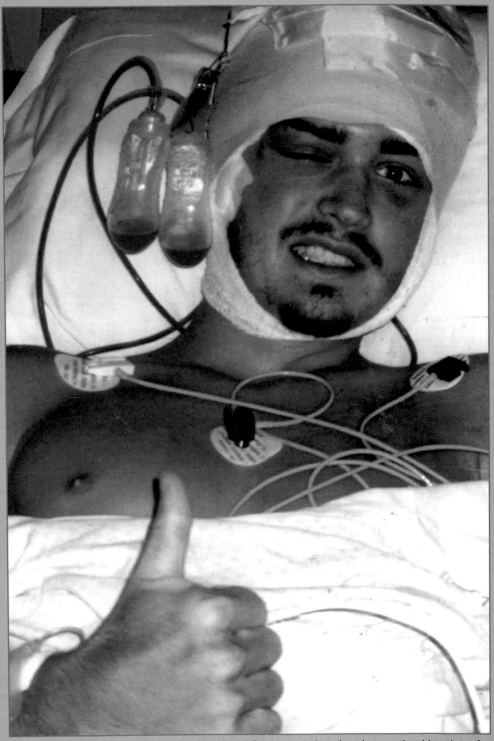

Gip gives his Shepherd Center angels a thumbs-up, thanking them for helping him celebrate his dad's birthday.

balloons, cards, birthday cake, and a choir of medical angels singing "Happy Birthday." Gip's face was beaming with pride. Mission accomplished! It was a beautiful experience, a birthday gift none of us will forget.

With tear-filled eyes, Richard leaned over and gently hugged Gip. He then looked back at all of us. Choked with emotion, Richard put his hand over his heart, signifying the words he was unable to speak: "thank you."

I wept as I stood at the foot of Gip's bed watching this magical moment unfold. I was immersed in a prayer of thanks, knowing that only God could bring such joy in a time of such suffering.

CHAPTER 17

Where Are You, God?

During the next few months, we battled the unknown. Each day was different from the one before. Some brought rays of hope; others were too unbearable to speak of. Even though we felt God's presence most of the time, there were still those agonizing moments when I cried out, asking Him where He was in all this.

As we recognized how weak we'd become, Richard and I began to pray for "eyes to see" and "ears to hear" to be sure we did not miss a single moment with God. We needed to feel His presence; we were lost without it.

We noticed that each time we found ourselves at a really low point and felt we couldn't go on, something would happen that lifted our spirits, comforting us with unexplainable peace. Wanting to have that feeling as often as possible, we began training ourselves to see the face of Jesus whenever, wherever, and however He appeared.

Sometimes it was through a nurturing nurse who stayed beyond her shift to offer a shoulder to lean on, or a doctor who stopped by after the usual rounds to bring some much-needed good news, or an early-morning prayer visit from a hospital chaplain who heard we'd been up all night with another crisis. Other times it was through a therapist who spent an extra hour helping Gip accomplish a goal he'd spent all day working on but had not yet achieved. There were moments we felt God's presence through a heartfelt glance of understanding clear across the cafeteria from another parent who knew of our pain.

Still other ways were through a tender voice message or a card in the mail, with just the right encouraging words to keep us going. There were times we came home to angel medallions secretly pinned to our pillows at night or a string of crosses carefully placed on our kitchen island. Our most cherished moment was when we saw the face of Jesus in Gip's face through a smile, when he had very little to smile about. And my personal favorite was through an unexpected middle-of-the-night "I love you, Mom" that came long after I thought Gip was asleep.

We also sensed God's presence through simple acts of kindness such as our lawn being mowed, our laundry being washed, or our house being cleaned. As crazy as it sounds, I still worried about such things during our long, quiet hours at the hospital. It's hard to turn your brain off simple worries, even when they've been trumped by major ones.

Many times we were at the end of our ropes and no one was around. That's when God's presence seemed the strongest. We found that as long as we turned to God for His strength—instead of trying to handle things with our human weakness—we could feel His peace seeping into our souls.

Recognizing God, in His many forms and through His many works, helped deepen our faith as His existence became more and more apparent. Our awareness of this helped provide us with the evidence we all crave that God really does exist. Let me tell you, for anyone who has ever doubted, He exists!

CHAPTER 18

Therapy

Gip with his beloved dog, Yeller.

Man's Best Friend

About two and a half months into Gip's recovery, the doctors allowed us to take him outside in his wheelchair for some fresh air. There is a courtyard on the hospital grounds where patients and their families meet for a change of scenery. Everyone knew how much Gip missed his dog, Yeller. So when the doctors gave us the green light to bring her to Shepherd Center for a little outside visit, we were thrilled.

The day was finally here. It was a beautiful Sunday afternoon, perfect weather for an outing with our dog. Richard and Taylor gave Yeller a bath, spruced her up for her big reunion, and drove straight to Shepherd Center. Once there, they got her settled down in the courtyard, had the camera ready to capture this wonderful Kodak moment, and called us to come out.

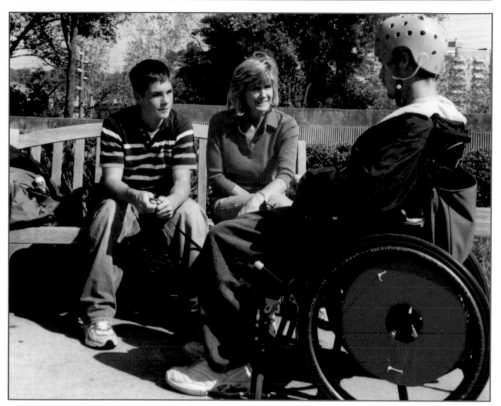

Gip sharing a story with Beth and Taylor.

Several of Gip's nurses and therapists helped me get Gip dressed and into his wheelchair. They hooked his IV to a traveling pole, connected it to the wheelchair, buckled him in, put on his TBI protective helmet, and sent us on our way. Gip did not have the ability to show much emotion at that time, but I could see the excitement in his eyes.

We had waited a long time for this wonderful moment between Gip and his "best friend." I wheeled him outside where Richard and Taylor were anxiously waiting with Yeller. What happened next took us all by surprise.

Yeller began to bark and growl at Gip, something she had never done before. She would not go near him and kept edging away as we struggled to keep her at Gip's side by pulling on her collar and leash. It was clear that Yeller did not recognize Gip.

That thought had never crossed our minds. It hadn't occurred to us that she wouldn't know *her* best friend. But clearly she didn't. She continued growling and tried to bolt as we forcibly held her next to Gip's wheelchair so he could pet her.

Gradually we came to understand what was wrong. Dogs know us by our scent. With all the medicines Gip was taking, his scent was distorted and unrecognizable. His looks were completely different as well. By this time, Gip had lost nearly seventy pounds. He was very pale, and he had a full beard. Wearing a helmet and sitting in a wheelchair, he was barely able to move around. Gip's voice sounded different as well, as he was too weak to speak with much volume or excitement. Yeller simply did not know who Gip was.

The look in Gip's eyes was enough to break anyone's heart. He knew Yeller did not recognize him. He didn't speak, just slumped over in his chair with a blank stare. After a few minutes, Gip quietly asked Richard to take him back to his room.

We tried every way we knew to entice Yeller to come near Gip and let him pet her, but she would have no part of that. We were all heartbroken as Richard wheeled Gip back into the hospital. With tears in our eyes, Taylor and I gathered Yeller, her leash, and her toys and headed back home.

Everyone who knew us was saddened by Gip's experience with Yeller's first visit. Many offered to bring her back whenever it would help. We tried to get her to the hospital as often as we could. But it didn't always work out well.

It took quite a few visits, but eventually Yeller began warming up to Gip. Perhaps she believed she was making a new friend. Or perhaps at last she realized that Gip was indeed her old friend, one and the same.

Yeller, after trying to remember Gip, finally warms up to him.

Music

When Gip had spells with severe headaches, his eyes became extremely sensitive to light. That made it impossible for him to watch television or movies to help pass the time. During one of his setbacks, Gip had to sit in the dark for more than a week with nothing to divert his attention from the unbearable pain and devastating challenges he faced. As we sat quietly with Gip through this time of darkness, we talked about what great things he would do once he was out of the hospital. We tried to speak about the future and how awesome things were going to be once he recovered. But there were many long periods of sadness for all of us.

One thing that helped pass the time was a gift from Gip's boss. During high school, Gip worked at a landscaping company. He and his boss, Randy Meyer, became good friends. Randy played CDs at work all the time, and he and Gip would often talk about their love of music and favorite songs. When Randy heard about Gip being "in the dark," he immediately began making CDs filled with songs he knew Gip enjoyed. He then came to the hospital and surprised Gip with a bagful of homemade CDs. Gip listened to them day and night.

At the time, Gip didn't have the strength to belt it out, but I could see the joy in his face as he mouthed the words to each song. That gift of music therapy was a timely blessing, and it helped keep Gip's mind occupied. Having listened to these CDs for so long, we all knew the lyrics to every song. As Gip began to feel better, he even started playing along with the band—with his "air guitar!"

Prayer

Our family has always believed in the power of prayer, but this was a test of faith like no other. *Everything* was at stake here, and we had to pray with conviction like never before. That doesn't mean we turned our worries over to God and went about our merry way. I wish! No, we are human. We had our share of weak moments.

We had to get past all the "what if" questions that seemed to consume our every thought. But even the worst "what if" question—the one we most feared—the "what if he doesn't make it?" question, could be answered by the truth of God's word that He will get us through it. That truth became our safety net. So we learned to consciously convert our doubtful thoughts into prayer and lay our worries at the foot of the Cross every time they surfaced . . . every single time.

During the really dark periods, Chuck came to the hospital and spent hours with Gip trying to lift his spirits. He told jokes, reminisced about their

Young Life club and camp experiences, and shared all the latest football updates and stories he could think of. When Gip's pain was so severe that he couldn't handle the light, Chuck sat in the darkness with him. Sometimes Gip didn't really feel like talking but wanted someone there. Chuck knew it and stayed because of it. As Gip dozed off, Chuck stood at his bedside and prayed over him.

Throughout Gip's recovery, Chuck was often the only one who could encourage him to take one more step, eat one more bite, read one more sentence. Chuck spent countless hours with Gip in therapies. His humor kept Gip upbeat even in times of total despair. He sometimes threatened to inflict some of his old football coaching workouts if Gip didn't work harder, eat more, or finish his daily tasks. All the while, Chuck continued to send out prayer request emails for Gip's every need.

Having been Gip's football coach in high school, Chuck knew how to motivate and inspire. But he was taking on a whole different kind of coaching role with this. He was now a "life" coach with a lot more at stake than a winning title.

The friendship they had before cannot compare to the brotherhood they built during those tough times. It was heartwarming to watch them get through it together.

Our amazing church pastors, Father Fred Wendel and Father Eric Hill, stopped by on a regular basis. They offered not only prayer support but humor as well, and Gip loved that! We built quite a bond with them and were continually lifted by their presence. And of course, Dr. Leslie was never far away, and we could always count on him for some comical wit to brighten our day. But mostly we found comfort in his words of wisdom and his treasured prayers. We also received countless visits from hospital chaplains, as well as pastors and ministers from other churches in our community.

It's amazing how many different church families and denominations bonded together to lift Gip in prayer. As the Scripture says, *"For where two or three have gathered together in My name, I am there in their midst"* (Matthew 18:20). We'll never know just how many gathered in His Name to pray for our son, but we'll be forever grateful that they did.

CHAPTER 19

One Step Forward, Three Steps Back

During the first three months of Gip's recovery, we seemed to be on a constant roller coaster. One day therapists were talking about Gip going home soon, and the next day the bottom would fall out, and we found ourselves back to square one. On several occasions, Gip's body shut down from infections and high fevers. And suddenly, he was at death's door again, being rushed into yet another surgery. The fear was crippling at times.

Some of Gip's surgeries were, understandably, related to his brain injury. He suffered from a severe case of hydrocephalus—a buildup of cerebrospinal fluid (CSF) inside the skull, which leads to brain swelling, debilitating headaches, and sometimes death. Due to the increased, chronic intracranial pressure, they had to surgically insert a catheter (known as a lumbar-peritoneal shunt) into his spine to help redirect the flow of spinal fluid from his brain through a cavity in his abdomen area where it can be better absorbed. That's my "laymen's terms" explanation.

In addition, Gip had to deal with the continual breakdown and reopening of his wound. This led to serious infections and often to more surgeries. He suffered from pneumonia several times and had to have breathing treatments; on other occasions, his lungs collapsed. He also had to have surgery on his jaw, which was damaged from the impact of his fall after he was shot. That was one reason Gip lost so much weight. His jaw caused such severe pain that he had difficulty eating. That tremendous weight loss led to even more concerns about Gip's overall health. He needed another surgery to insert a feeding tube to provide nutrients his body was lacking. Unfortunately, even that didn't work too well, as he continued to throw up for several months from the pain and stress on his body.

Another concern was the metal in Gip's head; hundreds of birdshot pellets remain embedded in his skull and brain. In addition to the threat of infections, he could not have an MRI scan (magnetic resonance imaging) because the pellets could move under the magnetic scan, causing further damage. Doctors were able to order CT scans on his head, but often the clarity of those tests was severely altered as well by the prism-like reflections bouncing off the birdshot. Without the benefit of these scans, it was difficult to make an accurate diagnosis of his ever-changing medical condition. Because of this, many of Gip's surgeries were exploratory.

Before each surgery, Richard and I had to sign those dreaded hospital consent forms. It wasn't enough that we signed the papers giving our permission for the procedures; the law required that the staff review the risks involved and verify that we understood them. Even though Gip had many operations, we never became numb to those cutting "risk" words. Each time they explained the dangers involved, it burned a hole in our hearts like a raging fire. Several times I had to walk out of the room, insisting that Richard sign the papers by himself. I simply couldn't bear to listen to it anymore.

Surgery after surgery, we found ourselves staring at the clock, painfully waiting for time to pass. When the expected finish time arrived, we anxiously focused our sights on the surgical unit doors. Each time they opened, our hearts jumped out of our chests, and we jumped out of our chairs.

Many hospital procedures took place at the same time, so the doors opened often. When our surgeon came out, we locked onto his facial expression right away, searching for glimmers of hope, good news, and surgical success. With adrenaline surging, we rushed to meet the doctor at the doorway, unable to wait until he reached us.

Having been through this waiting stage so many times, we had learned that some procedures took longer than originally anticipated. But one of Gip's surgeries was projected to take approximately two to three hours and ended up lasting almost thirteen hours! The day turned into night as we melted into our chairs, waiting and praying.

The surgeon sent several messages to us throughout the day to let us know that Gip was stable but still in surgery for a while longer. However, as time went on the messages were not informing us that things were stable but rather that there were complications.

Finally, the surgery was over, and the doctors came out and gave us the good news that Gip was stable, but also the grim news that they were running out of options to repair his wound. His scalp and tissues had become so fragile and tattered that the area would not stay sealed. Without closure, Gip faced more life-threatening complications. The doctors were able to cover the wound that day, but there was great concern that it would open again, and that meant more drastic measures would need to be taken. It was frightening to contemplate what those drastic measures would be.

We were concerned not only about the surgeries themselves but about the after-effects they would have. Each surgery set Gip back a bit—sometimes much more than a bit. He fought his way through months of therapies and was making great progress. But after every surgery, he found himself having to start over in many ways. It was like climbing an endless staircase. It's difficult to work that hard and see no lasting progress. But Gip was determined, and giving up was never an option.

Many times the physicians and therapists told us that Gip's perseverance amazed them. Richard and I would smile knowing that Gip's namesake—Richard's dad, "Big Gip," also known as "Poppi" by his four grandchildren—was a huge influence in Gip's approach to any battle in sports or in life. Having been a national Golden Gloves boxer and a professional minor league baseball player during the 1940's, "Big Gip" learned many lessons about working hard, pushing through pain, and getting up after being knocked down. He shared those lessons with Richard, who in turn passed them on to our sons, Gip and Taylor.

We certainly didn't think Gip would need to call on those lessons to this extent, but we were grateful they were already in place when he needed the extra push. Having been in athletics himself since Little League years, Gip realized that you can't stop trying just because you're tired or have had a setback with an injury. He was well aware that success in any challenge comes with hard work. He knew that winners never give up, and he did not want to lose his game of survival. So he pushed and pushed and pushed some more.

During the middle of his recovery's third month, Gip's wound closure was holding up fairly well, and he was once again progressing in his therapies. He was learning to read and write again and working on his comprehension and attention span. His short-term memory loss also seemed to be waning. He was still in a wheelchair most of the time because his body was so weak, but he was able to walk the hallways several times a day with a walker.

am proud of Gip and the way he has fought through and never given up. By example, he's taught me lessons that I'll take with me for the rest of my life. As a family, we've had some pretty tough times. But as Christians, we've grown through it. My mom and dad still amaze me the way they kept our family strong no matter what. Prayer is the most powerful gift we have, and I am blessed and thankful that God has taught me that.

—Taylor Gayle, Gip's younger brother

It wasn't easy to overcome the frequent setbacks. We became keenly aware that Gip was "reading our faces" to determine how he was doing. He needed to see hope from us to keep fighting as hard as he had to fight. So Richard and I took a deep breath every morning as we strategically put on our game faces. Day after day, we walked into Gip's hospital room with smiles on our faces and our heads held high.

It may seem like we weren't dealing with reality, possibly even losing ourselves in denial. Perhaps we were. But it was critical for our survival to wear the face of faith, not the face of fear.

Amazingly, that mask began to fool even us. The more we pretended to be strong, the stronger we seemed to get. We had to hold on to hope and believe what we say we believe, that *The spirit of God within us is greater than any challenge outside of us."*

CHAPTER 20

Time for the Truth

As we continued this crazy ride of good days and bad days, we shielded Taylor from as much as we possibly could. It's not that we intended to keep everything from him, but we were very cautious about what we told him and when.

There were times we didn't tell Taylor about Gip's critical situations because we knew he had a test at school the next day or a big game that night. When we did tell him about things, we chose our words carefully, so as not to alarm him too much. Looking back, I see that perhaps we were protecting ourselves as much as we were protecting Taylor.

Whenever an emergency arose, I called Jan, Taylor's second mom. I'd tell her what happened, and she would take care of things from there. When school or ball practice was over, Jan would pick Taylor up, telling him he would be staying with them that night. This happened so often that Taylor kept clothes at both houses, just in case. Fortunately, Taylor felt very at home with the Isbill family, so he never minded staying with them. Besides, Mama Jan is a great cook!

Typically, I'd call Taylor later in the evening and make excuses for my absence, such as having a hair appointment. Ha! What a stretch *that* was. A trip to the salon had become a thing of the past for me. Having highlighted my hair for the past twenty-plus years, hoping never again to show my natural color, all of a sudden it was rearing its ugly head. I now had a lovely trio of colors: my grown-out highlights, the roots of my natural color, and some newly acquired (and hard earned!) grey hair. Not exactly a salon special.

One evening after a harrowing day of setbacks, meeting with doctor after doctor to find new plans to handle new problems, Richard practically forced me out the door and sent me home. I was clearly at the end of my rope. As I drove out of the hospital parking lot, I picked up my phone to call Jan for help. But my heart ached to see Taylor. I desperately needed to hold him in my arms and love on him. I took a deep breath and put the phone down, thinking I could handle the pressure.

With each passing mile, I prayed for peace as I tried to keep it together. The moment I walked in the door, Taylor greeted me with a warm hug. Already I was beginning to lose it but somehow held back the tears. We ate dinner together and chatted for a while about the happenings of his day.

Taylor always asked how Gip was doing, and I usually told him that Gip was doing much better, even if that was stretching the truth a bit. Taylor had seen what *not* doing better looked like, so I did my best to upgrade that image. Richard and I didn't want Taylor's burden to be any heavier than it had to be, so we tried to keep it light whenever possible.

We said our "good night's" and "I love you's," and Taylor went upstairs to bed—or so I thought.

I went into my bedroom, located on the first floor and a bit of a distance from Taylor's second-floor bedroom. I shut the door, crawled into bed, and called my twin sister, Kay. The moment I heard her voice, I broke down in tears. As close as we are, Kay knew my thoughts and fears before I even verbalized them. I wept as I began telling her about that day's crisis, sharing how frightened I was by it all. Minutes later, I heard a loud BAM! upstairs. I threw the phone down and flew up the stairs to see what happened.

I grabbed Taylor's bedroom door knob to rush in and check on him, but it was locked. Taylor had never locked his bedroom door before; it was a house rule to have no locked doors. I banged on the door, screaming, "Taylor, are you all right?"

"I'm fine, Mom," he said.

I pleaded with him to open the door, saying, "It doesn't sound like you're fine. Please let me in." We continued with this for a few more minutes until he finally opened the door.

"What's wrong?" I asked as I slowly entered his room.

"You haven't been telling me the truth!" he replied, with a grave look of disappointment.

Barely able to think of a reply, I looked at my precious child and said, "Please, son, let's talk about this." I moved closer, trying to lean in for a hug. But he was still upset and pulled away from my attempted embrace. Apparently, Taylor did not buy my act that night.

In our tug of war, we both just sort of fell onto his bed. He stared at the wall for a while. I sat next to him, praying silently for guidance. I knew then he must have come downstairs and overheard me crying on the phone with my sister. When he ran back to his room, he slammed the door behind him.

Like the rest of us, Taylor had reached his limit and was overwhelmed by the chaos in our lives. All the more reason we were trying to protect him.

Finally he said, "I heard you, Mom. I heard everything you said to Aunt Kay. I came downstairs to see if Dad was home yet, and I heard you tell her about Gip. I'm not a child, Mom. I want the truth. It's time for the truth!"

I took a deep breath, searching desperately for the right words to say to my hurting child. I realized he overheard enough to know that things were very critical for Gip. Plus, it was after midnight, and Richard was not home. Taylor knew that if we weren't both home by eleven o'clock at night, there was a serious situation with Gip, and that's why one of us was spending the night. He realized his dad was still at the hospital, and he knew what that meant. As much as we tried, we couldn't hide it all.

Maybe it *was* time for the truth. I reached over and hugged Taylor as I told him how sorry I was that he was hurting. I apologized for not telling him the whole truth. I explained how we wanted to spare him whatever heartache we could.

As crazy as it sounds, sometimes I didn't want to tell Taylor how bad things were because I was afraid that if I said the words out loud, I'd have to hear them myself. But it was time for all of us to face the truth; even *I* had to hear it.

I broke down as I told Taylor that Gip had another setback and that things were not going well. He looked up at me and said, "Mom, Gip's not going to die. He's going to recover. I know it. I just *know* it!"

It took my breath away. Had we just reversed roles? Who was the parent and who was the child here? I honestly don't know how long the pause was before I could speak. But I took another deep breath and hugged my precious son as hard as I could. I thanked him for his faith and told him how proud I was of him.

We talked about things a little more, and then we prayed together. I tried to remind him—and myself—that no matter what happened in our lives, God would take care of us. He hugged me back and said, "I know, Mom. You and Dad taught me that, remember?" I sank into his arms.

When we finished talking I tucked him into bed as I had so many times when he was a little boy. In many ways at that moment, he *was* a little boy. Even though he was fourteen years old and fighting to be treated like an adult, he didn't resist my mothering. I gently rubbed his back until he fell asleep. I prayed silently at his side for nearly an hour.

I sobbed as I thanked God for His strength and His light that had just shone through my baby, my fourteen-year-old, my wise-beyond-his-years young man, my Taylor. I then prayed for guidance on how to provide peace in our home as we dealt with such trauma in our lives.

The following morning as Taylor left for school, he asked if I heard from his dad about how Gip's night had gone. I didn't really have an update yet because Richard was still waiting for the doctor's morning rounds before he called me. The last we had spoken was at four o'clock in the morning, and Gip was stable, finally dozing off to sleep.

I knew Taylor was anxious to hear good news about Gip's condition. I could see it in his eyes and hear it in his voice. So I told him that Gip had done pretty well through the night and that things were already looking better.

I know what you're probably thinking, but my response was a bit of a knee-jerk reaction. I'm a mom, and we instinctively protect our young!

CHAPTER 21

Thanksgiving

As we neared the end of month three, Gip began to show remarkable improvement. The doctors and therapists were scheduling his discharge from Shepherd Center for the following Wednesday, the day before Thanksgiving. We were ecstatic! We contacted our family, and they began making arrangements to fly in for Gip's homecoming. We had a lot to be thankful for. This was going to be the greatest of all Thanksgivings.

Amidst our excitement over Gip's homecoming was anxiety about getting our house ready to accommodate his new needs. At Shepherd Center, we took a TBI course about family caretaking. Then we set up nursing staff for home visits to address the medical issues we weren't equipped to handle. We ordered a wheelchair and set up grab bars around the house and the bathrooms. In addition, Chuck was planning a homecoming celebration for Gip. He had everyone on standby, waiting for the details of Gip's discharge confirmation so they could move forward with the big event.

Then out of nowhere, on the Monday before Thanksgiving, Gip's mind and body shut down again. Suddenly he stopped talking to us. He began hallucinating and thrashing from side to side in his bed. Even though he couldn't speak, he was screaming at things that weren't there. They rushed him to the ICU floor and began running a battery of tests.

Gip had been doing so well that we were in shock at this turn of events. Nothing seemed to explain his bizarre behavior. His heart rate skyrocketed, and he began shaking uncontrollably. He looked at us with a blank stare as he gasped for air. The doctors forced us to leave the room as they frantically tended to our child.

I called Chuck, once again pleading for prayer support. He immediately sent out an email, and then he and Scott came straight to the hospital. It was a godsend to have them with us; this time we needed their physical help. Once Gip was stable, the doctors let us back in the room. But he was still convulsing, and we struggled to restrain him.

Chuck and Scott stood on either side of Gip's bed and firmly held his hands and legs down as he fought to breathe. He was suffering severe tachycardia, causing his heart to beat at an alarming rate. The doctors had him strapped down, but he was thrashing way beyond the power of the restraints to hold him.

As Gip caught his breath, he begged us to help him. Richard and I stood near the head of his bed doing our best to comfort him. Over and over, Chuck repeated, "Gip, God is with you, God is with you. Hang on, buddy, hang on!"

The doctors gave Gip some new medication, and it seemed to help calm him a bit. At that point we felt that Gip had finally stabilized. We thanked Chuck and Scott for their amazing help and sent them back to their families for the Thanksgiving holiday. But later, Gip's condition deteriorated even further. Ultimately, the doctors pushed Richard and me out of the room—*again*.

Our son was in serious trouble, and we all knew it. Richard and I sat on the floor just outside the door as we listened to them screaming STAT and CODE and all the horrifying words we couldn't bear to hear. We clung to each other, immersed in moaning prayers as we watched one doctor after another rush into the ICU. Nurses were rolling in crash carts, scan machines, heart resuscitators, and more. After about an hour, the neurosurgeon came to the hallway where Richard and I were sitting on the floor, curled up in each other's arms in total disbelief. When we saw the doctor coming, we quickly jumped to our feet.

He rubbed his forehead and clasped his hands together, not making any eye contact with us. With his head facing the floor, he struggled to say the words, "I'm afraid we're losing him." He then looked up and said, "Neurologically, Gip is deteriorating at an alarming rate. They're prepping him for surgery right now, but I've got to be honest with you. He's fading fast." With that, the doctor turned around and rushed back in the room.

Moments later, the ICU doors flew open, and a team of doctors and nurses came running down the hallway with our son on a gurney, rushing him into surgery. Dr. Leslie, of course, was at Gip's side. He motioned for us to follow as he hurriedly pushed the gurney, leading the way for Gip and the medical crew to reach the surgery unit. As much as he tried to hide it, we could see the heartache on Dr. Leslie's face. He knew just how bad things really were.

Four hospital aides ran in front of the gurney, ordering everyone in the hallways to move, "STAT!" They were literally pushing people out of the way to clear the halls so Gip could get through. As Richard and I were running behind this band of medical staff, we were shouting, "We love you, son. Don't give up. Please don't give up!" It was worse than a nightmare. It was unthinkable!

Just before they closed the surgery doors, we caught a glimpse of Gip's face. He couldn't speak, but we could see his eyes were focused on us. His stare penetrated our hearts like a knife in an open wound.

We called out to our son, reminding him that we loved him and that God was with him. Then came a loud crashing sound as the massive steel doors slammed shut. Once again our son was rushed into surgery. Once again we were left behind to wait. And once again . . . our world stopped.

The surgeons weren't sure what they were dealing with, so there was no estimated time frame for this surgery. We had no choice but to wait . . . and pray. As we sat in that too-familiar surgery waiting room, we called family and friends for more prayer support. Our pastor, Father Fred Wendel, who by that time had become like family to us, arrived in fewer than thirty minutes. Under normal driving conditions, that same trip would've taken him nearly an hour, but we believe he had wing-power getting him there! As he prayed with us, his soulful manner lifted our spirits, giving us the extra push we needed to hold on.

Soon, Chuck and Scott were back. They had become "frequent flyers" from home to hospital. Several family members were already in flight to Atlanta to celebrate Gip's previously scheduled homecoming and Thanksgiving. When they arrived, they found things drastically different than they expected.

Air had slowly leaked into Gip's brain through a tiny hole near his sinuses. It was not an easy thing to detect, especially without the aid of an MRI scan. But the brilliant surgeons caring for Gip, Dr. Chris Clare, Dr. Gary Gropper, and Dr. Arthur Simon, never gave up. They were able to find and repair the leak and ultimately saved our son's life.

During those arduous hours in the ICU waiting room, Dr. Leslie stopped by often to keep us posted on Gip's condition. He mainly wanted us to know that he was "there for us." Before Gip was rushed into surgery, Dr. Leslie had been at his side praying for yet another miracle. He knew Gip needed more than earthly medicine at that point. He told us how he literally held Gip's brain in his hand, as he prayed for God to send a heavenly angel to save Gip's life. With that, Dr. Leslie handed me a beautiful handmade angel doll. Tearfully I reached up and hugged him. Without saying a word, we both knew what that angel represented: the angel he prayed for—the angel we *all* prayed for. It was a gift like no other. I wept as I held it close to my heart.

Unfortunately, Gip's body continued to shut down. He was so frail at that point; his body was unable to function on its own. He lapsed into another coma and suffered one complication after another. Many feared he was too weak to fight back. Surrounded by nurses 24/7, he remained in critical condition, and we stayed at his side around the clock. It was heart-wrenching to think that Gip was fighting for his life, by the hour—again.

We were doing all we could to stay strong, but some days were nearly more than we could bear. We almost lost our son several times during this period. We were battling despair with every breath. Fortunately, my parents and my twin sister, Kay, and her kids were in town. It was a godsend to have them there for us, but mainly for Taylor. They helped keep him occupied as Richard and I desperately struggled to hold on.

After six days of nonstop bedside care, we were strongly encouraged by the doctors to go home and rest, at least for a few hours. Gip's condition had remained the same for a while, but ours was deteriorating by the minute. Finally, Richard and I gave in to their suggestions. We gathered our pillows, blankets, and makeshift bedding from the waiting room and drove home in the wee hours. We practically passed out as we slowly crawled into our own bed.

Richard woke up a few hours later with chest pains and a racing heart. He didn't want to wake me until it was time for our five o'clock morning hospital call to check on Gip. So he lay there quietly, trying to calm his pounding heart. He finally got out of bed, thinking that might help.

I was awakened by his fall against the bathroom door. I jumped out of bed and ran to our bathroom only to find my husband on the floor, gasping for air.

"I'm calling 911!" I screamed.

"There's no time. Take me to the hospital," he insisted.

I quickly grabbed my robe, and we hobbled out the door in boxers and bathrobes.

We had family in town, but it was barely five o'clock on a Sunday morning, so they were all sleeping. As I was practically carrying Richard out the door, I screamed up the stairs to my sister Kay to help me. She flew down the stairs, asking what happened.

I told her it appeared Richard was having a heart attack, and I was taking him to the hospital. At first she argued with me, insisting we call 911. But she quickly gave up once she saw Richard's determination to get to the car as he struggled to breathe.

In hindsight, I should never have driven Richard to the hospital in that condition. But—let's face it—neither of us had been in our right minds for quite some time.

Fortunately, we live only five minutes from our local hospital, Gwinnett Medical Center. But it seemed like forever before we got there. I drove to the emergency entrance and rushed in, shouting for help. Nurses ran to the car with a gurney and quickly pushed Richard into a room. He could barely move or speak but clutched my arm as he slowly managed to get the words out, "Go to Gip."

I didn't know what to do. How could I leave my husband as they were hooking him up to heart machines and giving him nitrates? I watched as nurses checked Richard's vital signs. I could see the readings; his heart was racing uncontrollably, and his blood pressure was off the charts. They pulled the drapes closed as they began shoving me out of the room. They said it appeared he was having a heart attack.

I stood there stunned, unable to react. This was unfathomable. My husband and son were both in serious trouble, and I couldn't seem to help either one. I felt like shutting down myself. As they pushed me into the hallway, I grabbed my cell phone and called Piedmont Hospital to check on Gip.

The ICU nurses told me that Gip had taken a bad turn and that the neurosurgeon had just been called. I ran back to the ER unit and began knocking on the door, begging to talk with someone. I needed to know how Richard was doing and to tell them that I had to leave. No one was answering. I began crying and shouting and banging on the doors as hard as I could with what little strength I had left. Finally, a nurse came to the hallway and very cautiously opened the door with little more than a slight crack between us.

She told me Richard was stable but that I wasn't allowed to see him yet. I gave her a quick overview of the chaos in our lives as I frantically wrote down my cell number. I asked her to please tell my husband that I was going to be with our son, Gip. With that I hurried to my car and headed to Gip's hospital, forty-five minutes away.

Given the lives we were leading at that time, I always kept a change of clothes in my car. Since I was wearing little more than a bathrobe when I rushed Richard to the hospital, I grabbed my extra clothes from the backseat and dressed as I drove.

Kay was at my house frantically waiting to hear from me. I called and gave her the update on Richard and Gip. I told her I was on my way to Piedmont Hospital and that I needed someone to be at Richard's side. She and the rest of my family immediately drove to Gwinnett Medical Center.

After checking on Richard at one hospital, my dad left to check on Gip at the other. Being a physician, he was able to get the inside scoop on both patients.

Upon my arrival at Piedmont Hospital, Gip was somewhat stable, but still in critical condition. As I stood next to his ICU bed, I took many deep breaths desperately trying to breathe in peace . . . *divine* peace. I was crumbling. I knew I wouldn't make it through this without completely turning my worries over to God. I shook as I tearfully whispered, "Please, God, please."

After speaking with Gip's doctors, my dad came to the ICU room to see me. He gently put his arm around me and told me that everything was going to be okay. He explained that Richard had suffered a severe anxiety attack, perhaps even a mild heart attack, but that he was recovering well. It was a frightening experience, but we were greatly relieved that he would be all right. I wept as I rested my head against Dad's strong shoulders.

A few minutes later, I called Chuck for more prayer support. He sent out yet another urgent prayer request, this time for both Gip and Richard. During the next few hours, Chuck had family and friends camped out at both hospitals.

Richard's doctors insisted that he continue to be monitored for a couple of days. So he had to remain hospitalized through the next day for some follow-up stress tests. He was released the following evening with strict instructions to "get plenty of rest and avoid stress."

Avoid stress? Are you kidding me? You almost have to laugh at that! Lord only knows we would not have come this far without finding humor along the way. Quite often ours was twisted humor, but quite medicinal nonetheless.

After two days of rest, the doctors allowed Richard to go to Gip's hospital for a short visit. By this time, Gip was regaining consciousness and asking for his dad. It was amazing how strong the bond between these two had become. Not seeing Richard for a couple of days really took an emotional toll on Gip. It was touching but heartbreaking to see how much he depended on his dad's presence for reassurance of his own.

Having family around helped us cope with all the confusion. It was hard to believe they had come in town originally to celebrate Gip's homecoming. Now their mission was to hold us together as our lives were falling apart again.

My mom has a vivacious and uplifting spirit about her. In good times that leads to a lot of fun and laughter. In times like these, it brings the positive aura we all need. No matter what, Mom has a way of making it all better.

Quite often she would take my hand and hold it as her fingers gently stroked back and forth. We talked when I felt up to it, but even during the silence she comforted me in a way that only a mother can. Having her next to me helped me believe things were going to be all right.

Our family had the shoulders we needed to lean on, the comfort we needed to carry us through, the solidity that Taylor looked for. Their presence was the assurance that we would get through this as a family, united as one. Despite the miles between them, Taylor is very close to his grandparents, aunts, uncles, and cousins. He often turned to them for support, and that blessed him and us as well.

Some of those days are a blur to me. My body was there, but my mind and heart were elsewhere. With one child in the hospital fighting for his life and my husband in another hospital with heart concerns, I reached a point so overwhelmingly bleak that shutting down seemed like a matter of self-preservation. So I did. For days, I lacked my usual energy, and I could barely bring myself to speak, even to the people who meant so much to us.

That leads me to a subject that came up over and over again, especially among the families we grew close to during our lengthy hospital stay. When you're hurting like we were and in immense despair beyond anything you can imagine, it's easy to find yourself wondering *why* this happened to you or your loved one. You might feel the need to blame someone or something for your suffering, perhaps even God. I'm human; I understand that feeling.

I don't dare answer for others on how they deal with such unbearable grief. I can only share how I dealt with it. My whole world was falling apart, and so was I. The pain went deep into the core of my soul. I knew I couldn't handle it alone. I needed God more than I had ever needed Him before. So I just couldn't harbor anger and disappointment against my only source of real comfort. I couldn't place blame on the same God who was holding my broken heart in the palm of His hands.

The Bible tells us we will go through trials and tribulations but that we do not go through them alone. I believe God helps us through every step of our journey, if we let Him. Turning to Him does not eliminate all pain and heartache, but it does offer peace, along with glimmers of hope, and that helps us hold on. I'm thankful my heart feels the way it does about our nurturing Father because it has allowed Him to enter our broken lives and heal us in ways only *He* can.

Chapter 22

Give Me a Break

Living far away from family made it difficult for them to be with us all the time. They were constantly searching for ways to bridge the gap. Everyone helped in whatever way they could by taking shifts visiting us, handling our business affairs, and reaching out to Taylor. But they also yearned to give us a break somehow, a reprieve from the traumatic stress we lived in 24/7.

Before Thanksgiving, when things had seemed to be getting much better for Gip, my brother Jimmy and my sister-in-law Lisa made plans to surprise our family with tickets to the upcoming Southeastern Conference (SEC) Football Championship Game. Our LSU Tigers were playing against the local Georgia Bulldogs, and the game was being held in Atlanta in early December.

Living in Georgia all these years, we had become big UGA fans. But not when they play against our beloved Tigers—then all bets are off! We *bleed* purple and gold. This was the second time LSU would play against UGA that year. LSU had beaten the Bulldogs during the regular season, but this time we were "goin' to the 'ship," and the game was to be played on Georgia's home turf. It just doesn't get more exciting than that.

With high hopes for Gip's continued improvement, Jimmy and Lisa bought the tickets. But when Gip's condition deteriorated at Thanksgiving time, it was clear he wouldn't be able to go anywhere. None of us would.

Weeks later, when the SEC game was about to be played, Jimmy and Lisa decided to come to Atlanta anyway so they could be there for us. No one had intentions of attending the game. But after they arrived, Gip began showing signs of improvement. After a lengthy discussion, the doctors assured us that Gip was stable enough for Richard to leave for a few hours, and they encouraged him to go to the game. Within minutes Taylor and Richard were changing into their LSU team attire and heading to the Georgia Dome.

I stayed with Gip, of course. He was in ICU, so there wasn't a television anywhere near us. But since Georgia was playing in this big game, there were many doctors and nurses keeping up with the score. As I sat next to Gip's hospital bed, they quietly shared game updates with me.

LSU was winning, and I was not humble at all around those Georgia Bulldog fans! Being in ICU, I had to contain myself and not cheer out loud like I wanted to. But every time our Tigers scored, I lunged from my chair and shamelessly did my Tiger happy dance. It was awesome to have something to divert *my* attention that night as well.

I found myself practically purring as I thought about the fun Richard and Taylor were having, being with family and watching our LSU team claim another victory. I couldn't help but think of how Richard had been yearning for some quality time with Taylor. So as I sat there that night, I thanked God for my family and for their precious gift—that much-needed break.

CHAPTER 23

Don't Judge a Book by Its Cover

Gip continued to lapse in and out of a comatose state for several weeks after Thanksgiving. As I sat next to his bed thinking of ways to lift his spirits, I remembered a painting of Jesus that he really liked. I wanted that spiritual image to be in his ICU room when he woke, but it was still on the nightstand back at Shepherd Center. So I headed over to get it.

A tunnel runs between Shepherd Center Rehabilitation Facility and Piedmont Hospital, where Gip was rushed into surgery many times. By God's grace, that tunnel-to-life was there when minutes counted. I shudder to think what we would have done without it. Someone's insight years ago saved our son's life—and many others.

Each time Gip had surgery at Piedmont Hospital, we continued to keep his room at Shepherd Center as our home base. But when his condition deteriorated to such an all-time low, our "base" was in question.

I walked through the tunnel that day, as I had many times before. But this time when I opened the door to Gip's room, I was stunned to see a stranger in his bed and a mother sitting in my bedside chair. I was so startled that I jumped back and apologized, saying I had walked into the wrong room by mistake.

I quickly closed the door only to realize that I had not been in the wrong room. I *was* in Gip's room—the room number was clearly posted on the door. Confused and upset, I raced down the hallway to the nurses' station. As I turned the corner, I could see the staff scrambling to find the head nurse.

I heard them whispering, "It's Gip's mom. What do we tell her?"

Before I could say a word, the head nurse gently took my arm and walked me into her office with two other nurses. "Beth," she said softly, "Please understand—we *had* to give Gip's room to another patient."

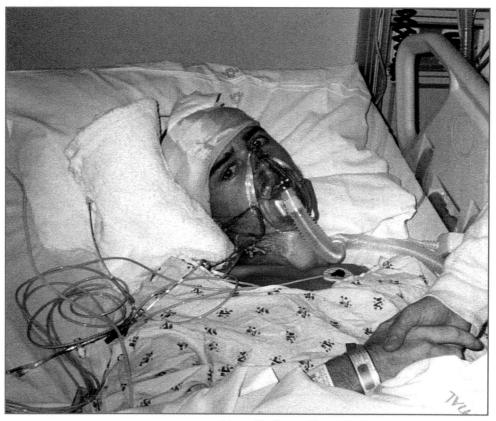

Gip at Piedmont Hospital shortly after Thanksgiving,
fighting for his life, determined to come back to us . . . again!

"But why?" I asked. "Gip's not finished with his therapies yet. Where will he go when he gets better?"

At that moment, I saw the grave expressions on their faces. They couldn't even look me in the eye, each of them staring at the floor. "Oh my gosh," I said. "You don't think Gip's coming back, do you?"

"We didn't say that, Beth," the head nurse quickly replied.

I was trembling as I said, "You didn't have to."

Because of Gip's absence for several weeks and his continuing critical condition, odds did not favor his return. There is an ongoing waiting list of patients who desperately need the help and hope that Shepherd Center offers, and time is of the essence in these cases. They had to offer his bed to someone who could actually use it. It was clearly understood that Shepherd would have a room for Gip when—*if*—he returned.

The nurses hugged me, and we all walked down the hallway to the storage room where they had placed Gip's belongings. They were going to help me find the Jesus painting I had gone there to retrieve.

But when they opened the door, I almost passed out at the sight of all the boxes, packed up and labeled with Gip's name on each one. It was an eerie sight to behold. I turned away and pretty much collapsed in the head nurse's arms.

As she held me up, she said, "We're so sorry, Beth. You know how much we love Gip. We love all of you."

I thanked her and responded with the same affection.

By this time tears were rushing down my cheeks. I began shaking uncontrollably and asked them to close the door, saying I couldn't bear to see those labeled boxes anymore. The head nurse put her arm around me again and said, "We're hurting *with* you, Beth. If there is anything we can do to help, anything at all." We hugged, and I went back to Piedmont to be with Gip.

Many of Gip's doctors, nurses, and therapists from Shepherd Center had come to Piedmont Hospital to see Gip and support us. Despite his intense and busy schedule, Dr. Leslie just couldn't seem to stay away. He had grown to love Gip like his own. His daily visits lifted our spirits more than he will ever know.

Gip's surgeons informed the ICU nurses to do whatever they could to make him as comfortable as possible. Many thought those might be his last days. Thankfully, they did not share that report with us. They did their jobs professionally and tried not to show the gloom and doom of reality. But no matter how much they sugarcoated their approach to caring for our child, we saw the subdued expressions on their faces. We knew.

Well, don't judge a book by its cover. Despite the horror of what we saw lying in that ICU bed and despite appearances that Gip would not make it through his latest battle, he did! After nearly a month in ICU, Gip was finally able to return to Shepherd Center.

When we wheeled him into his new room, his Shepherd Center family was waiting for his arrival, each one's eyes filled with tears of joy. They had draped a huge "Welcome Back Gipper" banner across the back window.

When Gip came to Shepherd Center for his rehabilitation, he was still severely injured. In the months that followed, he suffered complications and setbacks most people couldn't have survived. Gip faced many challenges throughout his recovery and was close to losing his life several times. One time we did lose him, and then the angels and the good Lord came and let us have him back, for which I will forever be thankful.

—Dr. Donald Leslie, *medical director of Shepherd Center, Atlanta, Georgia*

We were quite moved by this outpouring of affection. It was awesome to be back to our home-of-hope!

Gip had lost considerable ground in his recovery at that point, and we all knew it wouldn't be an easy task to return to his therapies. He had to start over again in many ways. But his therapists, nurses, and doctors were more determined than ever to get him back on track.

Gip worked hard, but I honestly believe that his loving staff worked even harder. The bond between them and our family is indescribable. Many times they've told us that Gip's return brought new life to their careers—and their faith.

CHAPTER 24

The Magic of Christmas

Christmas day at Shepherd Center with extended family,
including Honey, Pops, Aunt Susan, Uncle Brian, and the kids.

N̲o matter where we are or what's going on in our lives, when it's
Christmastime, things should be festive. They just should!

Well, that sounds great in theory but isn't always so easy to pull
off in reality. By this time, we were in full swing with Gip's therapies, and it
was all-consuming.

We were thankful to be back on the road to recovery, and things were
definitely improving. But our bodies and our minds were exhausted from
such a long journey.

Christmas was fast approaching and, understandably, we were not ready
for any form of celebration. We were practically living in a hospital and
had been for a long time at that point—nearly four months. Most of the
time, I didn't even know what day it was, let alone what season. Our focus
was on what each day would bring inside those hospital walls, not what
was going on in the outside world.

But Taylor was living in the outside world. So for him, evidence of Christmas was everywhere, except in his own home. One day while we were having one of our many family meals in the hospital cafeteria, Taylor casually asked if we were going to celebrate Christmas that year. I sank in my chair. I had lost all track of time. Millions of thoughts began racing through my mind. Christmas? When is it? Is it coming anytime soon?

I looked around the cafeteria and suddenly noticed Christmas trees and holly wreaths and candy canes everywhere. Hmmm, I thought. Guess it's not so far away.

After a long moment of puzzled thoughts, I tried to regain my composure. I looked back at Taylor and said we would certainly be celebrating the real meaning of Christmas, but we probably wouldn't be able to decorate or go gift shopping that year. Taylor understood. He hugged me and told me that it was all right. But I knew he couldn't help but be a little disappointed.

Chuck, with his uncanny radar, just happened to call right after my conversation with Taylor. I jokingly asked if he knew when Christmas was and told him that Taylor had asked if we were going to celebrate. Chuck didn't say a word to me but was already thinking of how he could help.

After our call, Chuck rallied the Young Life troops, and they spent all afternoon decorating the outside of our house. Late that night as we returned home from the hospital, we drove down our street and couldn't believe our eyes. Our home lit up the entire neighborhood. Words cannot begin to describe the joy in our hearts.

Taylor choked up a bit as he said, "Looks like our family is celebrating Christmas after all!" Now how do you thank someone for that?

Days later, my brother Tate flew in from Baton Rouge, and my Uncle Ed drove in from Nashville. In typical "let's get things done" fashion, the two walked in the door, assessed the situation, and went to work. They took care of a few household issues that needed to be addressed, and next thing I knew, they were off on a "Taylor extravaganza."

They started by taking him out for a nice steak dinner. Then they headed to the mall for a Christmas shopping spree. Taylor never asked for a thing, but they were determined to buy anything that seemed to put a smile on his face. He came home with new clothes, shoes, computer games, DVDs, and more. They also had a bag full of gifts for Gip. Suffice it to say that Taylor had never had such an indulgent Christmas before—or since!

Determined to make things as normal as possible, Tate and Uncle Ed set up our Christmas tree and brought down boxes of ornaments from the attic. They were waiting for us to come home so we could join in the tree decorating. But Gip was having a rough time that night, so Richard stayed at the hospital with him.

When I arrived home that evening, Christmas music filled the air, and ornaments were set out all over the family room, waiting to be hung. As we decorated our tree, we enjoyed the feeling of Christmas, reminiscing about the joys of past holidays.

In an effort to keep our spirits lifted, Tate and Uncle Ed started one of their famous (notorious) family joke-telling marathons. They told one funny story after another about our family shenanigans. Taylor and I laughed so hard it hurt. Since I was a character—or victim!—in some of their stories, Taylor seemed to laugh harder than I did. It was awesome to have our hearts and home filled with laughter again.

Later that evening, Uncle Ed called Richard, and they talked for over an hour. Knowing how tough things were, he knew Richard could use a listening ear. We've always been close to my Uncle Ed and his wife, BJ, so it was quite a lift to Richard's spirits to get that call. With all that was happening around us, it wasn't often that Richard had an opportunity to really open up, man to man. Thanks to Uncle Ed's comforting manner and spiritual wisdom, Richard was able to rejuvenate and move on to the spirit of the season.

By the time Christmas Eve rolled around, we were ready for it. We had a fully decorated home *and* hospital room. Many friends sent Christmas gifts to Gip and to Taylor. My friend Cathy made an LSU Christmas tree for Gip's hospital room, complete with purple and gold ornaments, Mike the Tiger mascot ornaments, and a treetop golden angel to watch over Gip. With no sign of humility whatsoever, Gip showed off his LSU tree to all his Georgia friends.

Gip with Honey and Pops (Santa!) on Christmas day.

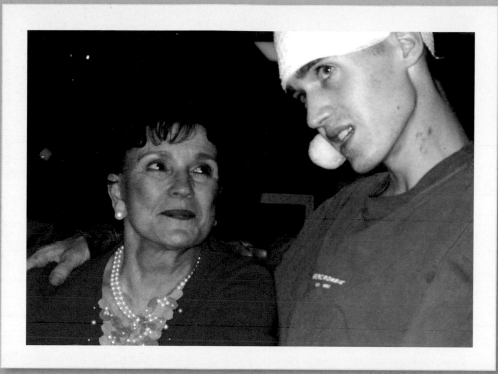

Gip with Honey, sharing a tender moment of gratitude.

Gip, Taylor, Beth, and Richard with Aunt Lisa, Uncle Jimmy, and their kids.

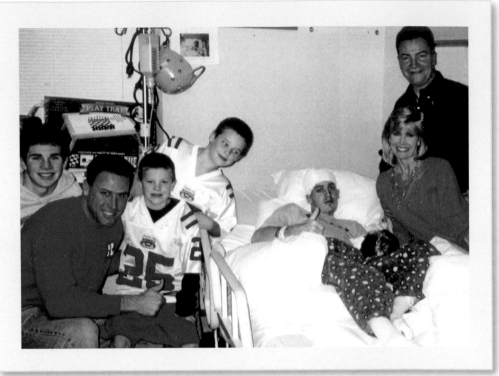

Chuck and sons, Chad & Caleb, visit Gip for Christmas
wearing their LSU jerseys. A Christmas gift from Gip!

Our family rallied around us throughout the holidays. My devoted parents once again drove in from Louisiana. My sister Susan and her husband, Brian, and their three children (they have five now!) uprooted their family from Nashville, packed up all their Christmas gifts, and drove to Atlanta to be with us.

It was extremely difficult for them to just up and leave home at Christmastime, especially with young children who had been looking forward to all the holiday parties, plays, and pageants, not to mention Santa's upcoming visit. It was tough to explain why they were suddenly taking off, leaving their lives and their plans behind. But Susan and Brian made the decision to put their family's needs aside to nurture ours. Along the way, they assured their precious little ones that Santa would know where they were, come Christmas morning.

My brother Jimmy and his wife, Lisa, gathered their four children and headed our way as well. It was a nine-hour drive from Baton Rouge. With a family of six, that's not an easy task. They, too, had to change many plans in order to reroute their family to Atlanta for the holidays. But they did it.

Thanks to the sacrifices of our loving family, we had a very special Christmas celebration.

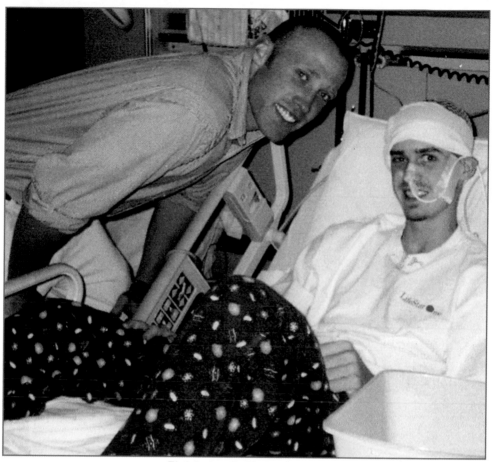

Gip's fraternity Big Brother, Eric Crenshaw, visits for Christmas.

With the hope of keeping things festive, my family did their best to carry on with some of our family traditions. As he does every year, my dad dressed up like Santa Claus. The rest of us put on our elf hats and paraded through the hospital hallways singing Christmas carols and wishing everyone a Merry Christmas.

My family is not exactly known for its quietness or subtlety, so there were many puzzled stares along the way. But most people knew of our need for being silly and carefree, so they quickly chimed in as our family parade passed by. It was Christmas, and we were alive to celebrate, so celebrate we did.

Shepherd Center allowed us to use its recreation room to have our family Christmas dinner. Before we served our meal, we bowed our heads as my dad led us in prayer. It was a Christmas like no other, and my dad offered a moving prayer to fit the occasion. He thanked God for showering our family with His amazing grace and for the gift of each day we have with Him, and with each other.

Gip visits with his lifelong friend Nick Disney.

Christmas in a hospital may not be what we had planned that year, but we were able to find blessings in the midst of our heartaches. There's so much to learn and gain from such an experience. Although a tough way to receive, it can be the gift of a lifetime if you do.

CHAPTER 25

Good Times

Sugar Bowl Party

College football's Sugar Bowl game was coming up in January, and our LSU Tigers were playing in it. It was being held at the Superdome in New Orleans, Louisiana, that year.

With his eternal optimism, Chuck made arrangements to take Gip and our family to the big game to watch LSU play Oklahoma for the BCS National Championship. Thanks to the generosity of many, Chuck had game tickets and a private plane ready and waiting in case there was even a remote chance that Gip could go.

Despite the positive thinking, Gip was clearly not well enough to leave the hospital, let alone travel or go out celebrating. It may seem crazy that we even dreamed of the possibility of going to that game. But hope—even far-fetched hope—kept us strong all along. Many things we hoped for did not come to pass, but it helped lift our spirits at the time, and I am thankful we never lost sight of that.

Still determined to make this big game special for Gip, Chuck quickly went to plan B. He called me one afternoon saying, "If I can't bring Gip to the Sugar Bowl, then I'll bring the Sugar Bowl to Gip. Is that okay?"

I said yes, but didn't really know what he meant.

Chuck made arrangements with the Shepherd Center staff to use its recreation area. He set up a tailgate-style party for Gip to watch the Sugar Bowl game with family and friends while still being near the medical care he needed. Chuck gathered some of Gip's high school football buddies to join us as we celebrated. Chuck's children pitched in by setting up a face-painting booth where we had our faces painted, Tiger style. LSU T-shirts and jerseys were passed out for everyone to wear.

Chuck's friend Poh served a Cajun feast that would knock the socks off even the finest of Louisiana chefs. We were eating spicy foods, celebrating our Louisiana heritage, and cheering on our Louisiana team. LSU banners, purple and gold streamers, and "Geaux Tigers" signs were hung all over the

Chuck's son, Chad, wheeling Gip into a surprise Sugar Bowl party
as Chuck's daughter, Jenna, looks on.

Gip and Chuck with family, YL friends, and high school football buddies, gathered to watch
LSU win the Sugar Bowl game for the National Championship!

Taylor with Chad and Caleb Scott, enjoying the cajun feast and the Tiger win.

room. Those of you who think I can't spell, look again. That's how we spell "go" in Louisiana. These are my roots!

Gip was thrilled about the opportunity to see so many friends at one time. But he was extremely tired and weak that day, and the doctors were concerned about him having so much stimulation. He had to wear a heart monitor to keep tabs on his heart rate. Throughout the night, nurses came in to check his vital signs and monitor readings.

At that time, Gip had very little stamina. His medical staff didn't think he would be able to stay awake past the first quarter. We were stunned at how well he was handling the excitement. It's not that he wasn't tired, because he very much was. But this was Gip, and this was his team. He was fighting just as hard as the Tigers to finish strong. He was in it to win it!

Gip managed to stay awake for the whole game and enjoyed every moment. He even pigged out on the fancy Cajun Specials. That's something we had not seen him do in a long time. It thrilled us to see signs of the old Gip.

It had been quite a year for LSU. The Tigers were kind of a Cinderella team—not really expected to have such a great season—but their hearts carried them to the big finish. Of course we knew that LSU had much more than just the players' hearts carrying them. They had the power of prayer backing them as well—just like our Gipper.

Gip with YL friend and mentor Scott Spears.

You see, knowing the joy it brought Gip to see his team win spurred many to begin praying for our Tigers. Well, LSU became the national champions that year. Since we don't know how the BCS (Bowl Championship Series) Poll delegates would rule on this "prayer assist" if they knew about it, we're keeping that information on the down low!

Fraternity Initiation

While still riding the high of our LSU national championship win, Gip received another exciting call. His Chi Phi fraternity president, Bobby Weir, called saying that the members wanted to have a special ceremony at the hospital to officially honor Gip and initiate him as one of their brothers. Eric Crenshaw extended his brotherhood even further by asking Gip to be his Little Brother. Even in that short period of time, Eric had already become a mentor to Gip.

Having been in college only three weeks before his accident, you wouldn't think Gip would have already built up such great friendships, but he had.

Beth with Eric Crenshaw, Gip's fraternity Big Brother (left), and
Bobby Weir, Chi Phi president.

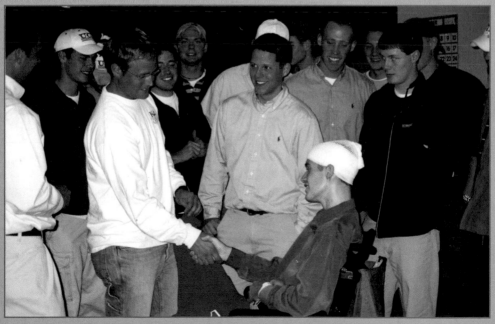

Chi Phi brothers congratulating Gip
and welcoming him into their brotherhood.

Those relationships grew stronger as these fine young men continued to visit Gip weekend after weekend, helping him through his recovery.

Gip tired easily in those days, and his mind often wandered in the middle of conversations. But despite his lack of energy and focus, these kids kept him well entertained. They brought normalcy back into his world, even in a hospital setting. It was a beautiful thing to behold.

Determined to include Gip in their brotherhood in whatever way they could, about thirty brothers drove to Atlanta for the big initiation. Given Gip's weak condition at that time, it wasn't easy for him to participate in much of anything. But with hearts of gold, these wonderful young men found a way to make a great celebration of it.

Before they began the ceremony, we were asked to leave the room, as only brothers were allowed to witness the secret handshakes and fraternity mysteries. Gip was thrilled to finally be unattended. They promised to take good care of him, and off they went into the secret room. As we waited for them to finish their private ceremony, we could hear peals of laughter, shouts, and cheers coming from the room. Those beautiful sounds of normalcy filled the hospital hallways and our hearts.

When they wheeled Gip out of their makeshift initiation room, they were all high-fiving each other and cheering for their new brother. Gip was sporting his million-dollar smile, and we were busting at the seams with joy. As he proudly held up his Chi Phi fraternity pin and jersey, we all began cheering.

Gip celebrating with his brothers after being
formally initiated into the Chi Phi fraternity.

Taylor thanking Gip's friend Ryan Hamil for his Chi Phi fraternity pin,
which identified Taylor as an honorary Little Brother.

After adding Gip to their private membership, the brothers were also kind enough to include Taylor in their celebration. One of Gip's good friends, Ryan Hamil, suggested that they name Taylor an honorary Little Brother. In an unprecedented act, they went back behind closed doors for yet another private ceremony, this time for Taylor. Ryan even offered his personal fraternity pin for Taylor to keep as a memento. It touched our hearts to see both our sons so celebrated.

Every one of those young men was beaming with pride. It told more of their character than they will ever realize. We were and still are very proud to know and love them.

CHAPTER 26

Doctor of Doom

Even though we were enjoying a few crowning moments with Christmas, football parties, and fraternity initiations, Gip was still suffering with major health issues. Unfortunately, his wound continued to reopen, and it was becoming imperative that we find a permanent solution to keep it closed.

The week after Gip's fraternity initiation, he had an appointment with a new specialist. This doctor came highly recommended, so we'd built up high hopes that he would have the answers we'd been praying for. As we wheeled Gip into the examining room, Richard and I glanced at each other with concerned but hopeful expressions, desperate to hear promising solutions for Gip's unique needs.

When the surgeon walked in, he did not introduce himself. He immediately began examining Gip's head and writing notes in his chart. He called the nurse in, and they began swabbing Gip's wound area to run lab cultures. The doctor asked us if we had Gip's medical records, and we handed over the large stack of charts from Gip's previous surgeries and medical care. He casually glanced over the documents and then tossed them on the examining table as if they were irrelevant.

When we tried to ask questions, he shushed us. Yes, he actually shushed us. He then looked at us with a very serious expression and said that he was the only doctor who could save Gip's life. He told us we got there just in time. He explained in great detail how his extensive training made him more qualified than any other doctor to help with these rare types of medical cases.

As he continued his narcissistic monologue, he told us that his state-of-the-art surgery would close Gip's wound, but that it would not safeguard his brain and he would have to wear a helmet for the rest of his life. He went on to say that we made a huge mistake by giving our son false hopes of recovery and that we should be ashamed of ourselves for that.

The venom flew out of his mouth so quickly we didn't have time to react before his vicious words left their mark. As soon as we caught our breath,

Richard and I glanced at each other with that "Are you for real?" expression, and Richard immediately began to wheel Gip out of the room. But the wheelchair locked up, and Richard was struggling to get Gip out the doorway. So he quickly leaned over to the doctor's ear. Speaking firmly but quietly so as not to cause alarm to Gip, Richard very clearly told the doctor that this meeting was over. With that, I grabbed Gip's medical records, and Richard and I lifted Gip and his wheelchair through the doorway and left.

Unfortunately, the damage was done. Gip heard and understood everything the doctor said. It all happened so fast, we couldn't stop it before it got ugly. As we hurriedly maneuvered Gip's wheelchair out of the office, we noticed tears streaming down his cheeks. It broke our hearts to see him hurting like this. We explained that this doctor had a clear case of the God complex, and sadly, we were his victims that day. We assured Gip there was much more hope than this doctor of doom was conveying and that God would soon lead us to the right doctors.

This was supposed to be a consultation only, a chance to discuss what this new specialist thought could be done to help our son. We thought this was going to be a huge step forward in Gip's recovery. But we soon realized that this doctor was not looking to help Gip. In some twisted way, he was in this for himself.

When we got back to Shepherd Center, the nurses asked us how the appointment went with the new doctor. Before we could respond, Gip looked at them and said, "I don't care what that doctor says—I *will* recover!"

I can barely talk about this part of our journey without feeling the rage all over again. If we hadn't had so much on our plates at that time, we probably would've done more than just leave. But we knew we couldn't stay focused on that doctor or his misdiagnosis. Gip's needs were way too critical and immediate; we had to put our time and energy into searching for the *right* doctors.

Fortunately, most of the doctors we came in contact with were angels in Gip's recovery and in our lives. We've seen many physicians and surgeons over the years and have several doctors in our family. So we've witnessed what *real* doctors are all about: men and women who've spent lifetimes studying and researching ways to offer hope, help, and healing to hurting families. They've earned our respect, and we will forever hold them in high regard for all they are to so many.

For the time being, Gip's wound had to remain open while our *real* doctors researched the best way to proceed. It wasn't easy to leave things unresolved, but we knew we were in good hands, and we had to trust that God would soon lead us to the right specialists.

CHAPTER 27

It Takes a Village

As we moved into the fifth month of Gip's recovery, we were still searching for solutions to permanently close his wound. That need became even more urgent as a potentially lethal staph infection—MRSA (methicillin-resistant staphylococcus aureus)—was now flourishing in Gip's brain. We were painfully aware that time was running out to seal the wound.

That search, along with his continued therapies, kept our lives in a chaotic mode. As much as I tried to wear rose-colored glasses, I knew what the reality was—I was living it. Without the help of family and friends, we simply would not have made it through this.

Gip's hospital ordeal turned into a lengthy stay, longer than anyone had anticipated. But our earthly angels filled in the gaps of our lives. Some of my very close friends from my previous job of seven years—Joy, Robin, Pam, Sherry, Cindy, and Carrie, who are lovingly referred to as my Ya-Ya's—organized a meals-on-wheels schedule to feed Taylor that lasted for more than five months. They rallied the troops from our coworkers, church friends, neighbors, our kids' ball team families, and even teachers and coaches' families. It was amazing how day after day, week after week, and month after month, the meals just kept coming. Taylor was eating like a king, and it certainly put a smile on his face.

By the time we left the hospital each night, we were exhausted physically, mentally, and emotionally. We were thankful to have dinner already prepared. We were also grateful for all the cards and letters in the mail each day. The food recharged our bodies, and the encouraging words recharged our souls. Both helped us face the following day's challenges. Many times we told friends to stop bringing meals, saying that it really wasn't necessary, that we had things under control. Thankfully they didn't listen, because clearly we had nothing under control. But through the kindness of many, the village did.

Taylor was involved in three sports during his freshman year in high school: football, wrestling, and baseball. That turned out to be a saving grace for our whole family. Instead of coming home to an empty house every day after school at two thirty, he stayed at school until six or six thirty in the evening for his team practices. When he got home, he ate his wonderful home-cooked meal, hopped in the shower, and then began his homework while waiting for at least one of us to come home.

My days typically started at five o'clock in the morning with a phone call to Shepherd Center to find out how Gip's night had gone, shortly followed by my arrival there, usually by six thirty. I stayed until Richard arrived each evening.

Richard's days were even longer. He went to work at the crack of dawn, typically driving an hour and a half to the job site and then another two hours to Shepherd Center every evening to spend time with Gip. When he arrived, we'd have our little medical chat about the day's happenings, and I'd head home to be with Taylor. By nine thirty at night, Richard usually headed home, too.

Once home, Richard and I put all the focus on Taylor's life—talking about what he had going on and how his day had been. I'm not saying we perfected this switch in gears each day, but we tried our best. Taylor is a very strong young man and was holding up remarkably well, all things considered. But it pained us knowing the heartache he had to bear. Watching how fast he was forced to grow up still tugs on our heartstrings.

On weekends we brought Taylor to visit Gip. But Gip was usually so exhausted from his weeklong therapies that he slept most of the time. We tried to make it a positive experience and have some form of uplifting family time together, but it wasn't easy. We could see the pain in Taylor's eyes as he watched his big brother struggle to do even the simplest tasks. Taylor's visits were rarely what we hoped they would be.

It was a daily struggle trying to be in two places at once. When we were with Gip, we worried about Taylor. When we were with Taylor, we worried about Gip. We tried to arrange our schedules so we could be parents to *both* our children. Gip's needs were more obvious to the naked eye, but Taylor needed us, too, and we needed him. Lord only knows what must have been going through his precious young mind. Taylor was trying to keep it together for us just as much as were trying to keep it together for him.

Richard and I took turns attending as many of Taylor's sporting events as we could. But we both missed when Gip's condition was critical. We have always enjoyed being a part of our sons' activities, so it broke our hearts not to be there for Taylor.

But our pain was eased many times by the love and support of our beloved community. Beyond the amazing meals-on-wheels angels and Taylor's awesome second family, many other friends in the "village" stepped in to help take care of Taylor. They went to his sporting events, cheering him on when we weren't able. They gave him rides to and from school and ball practices. They included him in their own family activities—taking him to movies or dinner at grandma's or just hanging out at the pool. In addition, many of Taylor's teachers and coaches pitched in to help in whatever ways they could. Many wonderful earthly angels went way beyond the call of duty, reaching out to help make Taylor's life a little more normal.

There was also the wonderful gift of Young Life ministry. Taylor had already seen the blessings it brought to Gip's life, so he was excited to be a part of it. He invited many friends to come to YL club, and together they enjoyed fun and fellowship as they grew in their faith. The new leader, Jeff Lewis, became quite a mentor to Taylor. Jeff was there for him during some really tough times in ways we couldn't be. We'll be forever grateful for that.

CHAPTER 28

Oh Say, Can You See?

Prior to his injury, Gip had 20/20 vision. After his accident, however, there were many concerns. In addition to the pellets in his skull and brain, there were numerous pellets still embedded in his face just below the skin, especially around his right eye.

At first, Gip's eyes were swollen shut from the trauma and the surgery. That made it difficult to know the extent of the damage done to his eye or his sight. With the emphasis on critical care to keep him alive at that time, Gip's eyesight was not the doctors' primary concern.

When we first asked about his sight, the doctors told us they would do all they could, but that his right eye area was severely damaged and he might lose his sight, if not the eye itself. This was devastating news. With all the other life-threatening issues Gip was facing, we tried not to let this weigh us down, but it never left our minds.

As swelling subsided, the doctors began testing Gip's vision. The nurses lifted his eyelid several times, and Gip told us that he could see us "just fine." But after a thorough eye exam by a specialist in Savannah, we were told that Gip's vision in his right eye was quite impaired. We were informed that the eye itself would be spared, but that he might require surgery to restore his sight.

Once we arrived at Shepherd Center, its staff, too, began testing Gip's vision. Each week they ran a gamut of exams on both eyes. Even though nothing medically had been done to correct his vision, his sight was improving dramatically on its own.

Nearly five months after his accident, the doctors felt that Gip was ready for a complete and in-depth sight evaluation. He met with a neuro-ophthalmologist to check all aspects of his vision. This specialist tested not only his vision's clarity but his eyes' capabilities as well, such as the speed of his reaction to light and motion and his peripheral visible awareness. Because these tests were so extensive, they took several hours to administer.

I remained in the waiting room as they thoroughly examined every component of Gip's vision. As I sat there, I couldn't help but wonder how he was doing. I watched through the closed glass doors that separated the staff from the waiting room and observed as they wheeled Gip from one testing room to another.

At one point, I saw several nurses looking at me through the glass doors. They had a stack of medical folders in their hands and began to point in my direction. Unsure if they were trying to signal me, I motioned with my hands on my chest as I mouthed the word "Me?" It appeared they didn't notice my gesture, and they went back to their desks.

Naturally, this concerned me, so I asked the receptionist if everything was all right. She excused herself to check with the nurses. Seconds later, two nurses peeked around the corner, smiled, and gave me a thumbs-up as they walked back to the testing area. I smiled and returned to my seat, trying to understand what it all meant. It seemed to be good news, so I felt relieved.

About thirty minutes later, I was called into the examining room to join Gip. As they were wheeling him in, the doctor had a big grin on her face. She said if she had not "seen it with her own eyes"—interesting choice of words from an eye doctor—she would not have believed it.

She had been reviewing Gip's medical records prior to his visit. Knowing his brain injury's extent and the physical damage to his eye area from the blast, she was prepared for a tough situation. She said she was shocked with Gip's test results. She looked at me and shrugged her shoulders as she told us that she repeated several tests to be certain there were no misinterpretations of them.

Several nurses walked in at that point to share in the joy. We were all rejoicing in this miracle. The doctor had tears in her eyes as she told me that Gip had perfect vision . . . again. She released him from all vision restrictions.

I hugged the doctor and each of the nurses. As I bent over Gip's wheelchair to give him a hug, I noticed that his return embrace lasted extra long. When I pulled away, I saw that he was a bit choked up.

I asked him if he was all right. He told me he had been praying about this neuro eye exam. Then he looked at me with a big smile on his face and said, "They told me my sight is good enough to drive, Mom. I'm going to drive again! Can you believe it?"

That's when I realized just how important that particular appointment was to Gip. He knew these exams were not only critical for his vision, but for his chances to one day drive again. That was Gip's goal for passing these tests.

CHAPTER 29

Home Sweet Home

Leaving the Nest

By this time, Gip had spent almost five months in the inpatient program, pretty much breaking Shepherd Center's existing resident record. He interacted with many other patients and even developed friendships with several. We, too, built bonds with the families we met. We were all in a difficult place in our lives, and we helped each other whenever and however we could. Their victories became our victories. Our victories became theirs. We cheered for each other in the good times and held each other up in the bad. It was therapeutic for all of us.

Once patients reach a certain recovery level, recreational therapists treat them to several mini field trips such as an afternoon at Walmart, dinner at a nearby restaurant, or a movie at a local theater. Patients look forward to these outings. Unfortunately, Gip was never able to participate because of his open wound. The risk was too great to take him outside the hospital. It was yet another reminder that his injuries were different from many other patients' and that his recovery would come with additional challenges because of it.

Due to his many setbacks, Gip's stay lasted longer than most. It was hard not to notice that patients who arrived long after Gip were leaving way before him. As wonderful as it was to see them celebrate their homecomings, it was difficult for us to watch others moving forward in their recoveries as Gip was often sliding backward in his.

But we couldn't let our disappointments cloud others' celebratory days. Despite his situation, Gip was always one of the first to wheel into their rooms to congratulate them and wish them well "out in the real world," as he would say.

Being in the hospital for such a long time was really tough. Each day seemed to take a little more out of us, and we found ourselves lost between what was normal and what was not. We dreamed of the day we could take *our* child home. We yearned for life's simple pleasures that we had once taken for granted.

Finally, after five long months, Gip was discharged from Shepherd Center. Words cannot possibly express how happy he was to be going home. We danced around his room, wheelchair and all, as he grinned from ear to ear with excitement. When the news spread, many other patients and their families stopped by to wish us luck and offer Gip a congratulatory high five.

On the morning we prepared to leave, Dr. Leslie, along with Gip's therapists and nurses, gathered in Gip's room to say their goodbyes. We had been there so long, they'd become like family to us and us to them.

LEFT: Dr. Donald Leslie saying goodbye to Gip and wishing him the very best.

BELOW: Gip with Margaret Sharp, his physical therapist.

Gip with Kathy Farris,
his occupational therapist.

With Jennifer Douglas,
his speech therapist.

With Brandi Bradford,
his therapist technician.

With Sean Burage,
his behavioral technician.

Dr. Leslie put his hand on Gip's shoulder and said, "I am proud of you, son, and thankful to God for your recovery. I'm glad you are able to go home, but I will miss your smiling face here at Shepherd." Gip thanked Dr. Leslie and shook his hand, and they both moved in for a warm embrace.

Dr. Leslie then turned to me with tears in his eyes. He gently took my hand as he softly said, "Anything . . . anything at all."

Unable to speak, I nodded my thank you. I hugged him and choked on my words as I whispered, "How can we ever repay you for what you've done for our child, for our family?"

Dr. Leslie turned around and smiled as he pointed to Gip and said, "You already have!"

The mood in the room was joyful, but tearful as well. Gip's therapists were overcome with emotion as they shared how grateful they were for this day of celebration—a day we had all feared might never come. Each one expressed thoughts about how proud they were of Gip's fight, his never-give-up attitude, and his joyful spirit.

As Gip thanked them, he hugged each one and told them he would miss them. They were his familiars, his roommates, his teammates. In many ways, he felt like he was leaving his best friends. In many ways, he was.

Shepherd Center had become our home. And I must admit I was a bit unsettled about leaving the calmness of its medical safety nets and venturing out on our own, where there were none.

Welcome Home, Gipper!

Once Chuck got the news that Gip was coming home, he set up a team to begin decorating our home and neighborhood. Banners displaying such messages as "Welcome Home, Gipper," "We Love You," and "You Are Our Hero" were proudly displayed up and down our street. There was a sign in every yard on the main street entering our subdivision with a message welcoming him back. Many of our friends had been at our side, riding out the storm with us. We were all excited to have the Gipper home.

Posters, streamers, and LSU decorations hung throughout our house. Chuck's personal favorite of all the décor was a huge banner hung across our foyer for all to see. It read, "Welcome Home PIG!" (Gip's name spelled backward). They had *way* too much fun joking around about that one! Our living room was filled with stuffed animals: tigers for LSU's mascot and pigs for, well, you know.

"Welcome Home Pig"

The freezer was full with Gip's favorite meals, just waiting for his appetite to return. Baskets were filled with prayer cards, prayer blankets, letters, and crosses to welcome him home. My friend Laura dropped off several bags of "doo rags," knowing Gip needed to wear head coverings during his healing stages.

Gip was grateful for all the attention, but it was a lot to absorb at one time, especially after being away for so long. He was trying to take it all in but was most anxious to get outside to see his dog. For Gip, being with Yeller was the homecoming highlight. From the minute he got home, the two were inseparable. Yeller had always enjoyed playing catch with Gip, so as soon as he went out on the deck, she ran to get her tennis ball for the big game. Gip was too weak to play the way he used to, but he still tried throwing the ball, and she joyfully retrieved it.

Yeller welcomes Gip home with a request to play a game of catch!

LEFT: Pops joins Gip in celebrating his homecoming.
RIGHT: Honey and Aunt Kay celebrate Gip's homecoming as well.

Gip and Taylor with Taylor's second family, the Isbills.

Chuck and sons with Gip and Taylor.

Nick Disney welcoming Gipper home.

It was interesting to watch Yeller as she became aware that Gip was still not himself. She whimpered as we helped him onto the sofa from his wheelchair. Her innate sense knew Gip was not well. Day after day, night after night, she sat patiently at his side, jumping up every time he so much as took a deep breath. We could tell she was on full alert, ready to serve at any time.

We teared up when we watched Yeller patiently wait for Gip to move his pillows around till he got comfortable. Once she felt Gip was settled, she would lift her paw and gently rest it on his hand. As he slept on the couch, Yeller slept next to him. She followed him around in his wheelchair and continued to "assist" when he was able to do his walking exercises. It touched our hearts to see Yeller help nurse Gip back to health with canine therapy.

Living in the hospital hadn't exactly presented many opportunities for Gip to be Gip. In a lot of ways, it was like being in a lab setting. He rarely showed signs of his old self. Because he'd been there so long, there were many things about Gip's personality we thought were lost forever. But re-

Gip settles in with Yeller, home at last!

turning to his familiar surroundings seemed to bring him back a little more each day.

As he eased into life at home, we began to see more and more of our Gipper. It was a slow return, but it was happening, and we celebrated every time we glimpsed a spark of our son's light.

Not on My Watch

It was wonderful to be back in our home environment. We felt such great relief to be reunited with our little family, all of us sleeping in our own beds, with no more daily commutes to the hospital, and our family of four living under the same roof again.

But after the initial hoopla ended, things got pretty rough. Gip had *so* many needs. Richard and I were terrified about how we were going to meet them. To this point, we had been surrounded by the security of nurses around the clock *and* around the corner. They were at our beck and call 24/7.

And now it was just us—Richard, Taylor, and me. We had no real medical training. And this was our child! What if something happened and we didn't know what to do? The pressure and fears were mounting. Rest became a thing of the past. When we did actually crawl into the bed, we slept with one eye open.

Gip still had a hole in his head, about the size of the palm of my hand. We knew he was going to need more surgeries, but until then we were responsible for his medical care. Before we left, Shepherd put Richard and me through an intensive medical training course on how to care for our child.

The doctors and nurses also reviewed Gip's medications, applications, dosages, and side effects to watch out for. The intense schedule and workload were enough to make a medical student quit the profession. But *we* couldn't quit. Our son's life was dependent on our taking care of him . . . *good* care of him.

A home health nurse came by daily to help change Gip's bandages. Other than that, we were on our own. Every morning before I wheeled Gip into our makeshift medical facility, I did my best to steady my trembling hands and hide my tear-filled eyes. I took a deep breath, put on my game face, and in we went.

I helped the nurse as she unwrapped Gip's head bandages, cleaned out the medical ointments around his dura (the brain's lining), and applied fresh medicines. How I didn't pass out from that sight is beyond me. We then rewrapped his head with fresh gauze, making sure not to apply too much pressure, as that could possibly cause brain damage or infection.

Keeping this work area clean was another battle. Everything had to be sterilized thoroughly prior to each dressing change. We turned off the air conditioning and closed the air vents before we began so as not to have any undue airflow. So many questions were running through my head: Was the air in our home clean enough? Did any of us have a cold coming on? Was my throbbing headache contagious or just something resulting from all the stress? Were our gloves too big? Might they slip while we were working around our son's brain? Did we secure our masks and gowns well enough to prevent germs from spreading?

This was not the typical recovery plan. Most TBI patients spend time at Shepherd's inpatient rehabilitation center, immediately followed by time at its outpatient facility, a satellite location a few miles away in Decatur, Georgia. This keeps the patient's momentum moving forward. But with Gip's open wound and the concerns of infection and further complications, he could not be released to his outpatient therapies until his wound was permanently closed. Since his next surgery was still in the research stage, his recovery faced another lengthy delay.

In order to maintain Gip's progress and not lose any ground, it was imperative that he continue his therapy routines at home. He had to remain mobile for several hours each day, continuing his workouts for all different muscle groups. We also needed to continue his cognitive stimuli. His therapists sent workbooks filled with speech and memory worksheets, along with a schedule to maintain daily improvements.

On top of these regimens, we also had the daunting daily tasks of a shower and three meals. Despite the problems it presented, Gip was supposed to do a lot of these things unassisted. Watching him struggle to accomplish even the simplest tasks was more than I could bear some days. Just taking a shower and getting dressed each day took him several hours.

Gip was still in a wheelchair most of the time, so getting him up and down was a challenge. I'm not a very large person, so lifting him was quite a feat. I was painfully aware that if he fell and hit his head, we were right back to square one—or worse.

Richard had to go to work and Taylor to school. So whatever Gip's needs, I had to find a way to meet them. There was nothing we could do to change that. When Gip needed to get in and out of the bed or wheelchair, go to the restroom, or go to a doctor's appointment, he couldn't do it alone.

Fatigue was setting in on all of us. There were days when I felt like crawling in a hole somewhere to nurse my own wounds.

But chop-chop—there's work to be done.

CHAPTER 30

One in a Million

In most situations, the phrase "one in a million" is considered to be quite a compliment. It's something many would love to have said about themselves. But not like this. This comment was used far too often referring to the uniqueness of Gip's medical condition. It was not a compliment at all. It defined the lack of common ground between his case and most others.

By this time, about six months had passed since Gip's accident. He had survived quite a few crises already and was finally home from the hospital. But he was nowhere near healed. He still had a life-threatening infection in his brain, and it was critical that it be treated and the wound closed safely and permanently.

The area of defect in Gip's skull was so large that it was difficult to compensate for without implanting a steel or synthetic plate of some kind. Typically that is what's done to take care of such a problem. Unfortunately, Gip was not a good candidate for this type of surgery. Given his weakened condition, the risk of infection and rejection of a foreign object was far too great. After numerous medical opinions, it was decided that the safest approach with the highest chance of success would be to use bone from Gip's own body to cover and close the wound.

Finding a specialist who could perform this type of surgery was no small task. The search was limited even more because Gip was too weak to travel far. That left us with fewer options, as it was clear we had to find someone nearby to help our son.

Many times we felt we were running out of options. I kept thinking about the scripture: *"Ask and it will be given to you; seek and you will find; knock and the door will be opened to you"* (Matthew 7:7). I had to believe my prayers were being heard. I tried to stay strong and have faith, but that was easier said than done sometimes.

Finally, after a long and wearying search by Dr. Leslie, along with my brother and dad (Dr. Jimmy Morris and Dr. Clifton Morris, both physicians in Louisiana), and the generous aid of their fellow doctors and friends Dr. Anthony Stephens and Dr. James Wade, we were able to find three highly trained specialists right here in Atlanta. We felt certain God's hand was in that.

The surgery would involve a craniofacial reconstructive plastic surgeon, Dr. Fernando Burstein; a microvascular reconstructive plastic surgeon, Dr. Franklyn Elliott; and a neurosurgeon, Dr. Roger Hudgins, all working together to rebuild Gip's skull. We met with these doctors and felt God's peace right away. Their bedside manner was incredibly compassionate; it was clear they were there to help Gip, not to pump up their own egos. They went to great lengths to explain the advantages and risks involved in this groundbreaking surgery designed especially for our child.

As the doctors expounded on their plan's details, we were overcome with emotion. It was hard to imagine so many different surgeries taking place simultaneously. Richard and I took several deep breaths as they reviewed what would prove to be a very delicate and intense surgical masterpiece.

The plan was to perform a "split-skull bone graft" surgery (my layman's term). In it, the craniofacial reconstructive plastic surgeon and the neurosurgeon would cut out and remove skull bone from the left side of Gip's head in a similar shape as the right side's missing part. They would then slice this piece into two layers and place half back on the left side and the other half over the right. That would give each side of Gip's skull only half the thickness of a normal skull bone, but it was better than no thickness at all.

Before they put the skull parts back in place, the neurosurgeon would need to remove Gip's dura—the brain's outer lining. This had already been removed twice in previous surgeries, with a pigskin substitute put in its place. But due to the seriousness of the MRSA infection in Gip's brain, the dura had to be replaced again, with yet another sterile, uncontaminated one. Hearing all this caused us great concern, as we knew that any maneuvering around the brain posed tremendous risks.

The microvascular reconstructive surgeon would be working on Gip as well. He would make an incision in Gip's stomach extending from his chest down to his navel to remove his *omentum,* a vascularized (blood-rich) membrane that drapes across the intestines. The surgeon would then carefully wrap the membrane around the skull bone graft as an omental free flap. The hope was that the vascular activity of the omentum would stimulate blood flow around the bone implants, helping them grow into one solid piece.

Once these surgeries were completed, the plastic surgeon would remove a section of skin from Gip's thigh and graft it onto his head to cover the free flap. Gip had already had several skin grafts taken from his legs in previous surgeries. This one was quite large, so the surgeons were running out of areas to graft. It sounds simple compared to the rest of the procedures going on, but there were many infection risks involved in this part of the surgery as well.

It was mind-boggling to process all this information. We were in awe and agony over the possibilities—and the risks. There were no guarantees. If things went well, this multisurgery would provide a solid layer of protection over Gip's brain—the answer we so desperately prayed for. If not, we were back to square one. In many ways, it was a gamble to go through with it and a gamble not to. We were in a catch-22 position with our son's life.

There was also great concern about whether Gip was strong enough to face such a complicated surgery. We sought many professional opinions during this search and solicited many prayers to guide us toward the right decision. Finally, we had to believe that our child had been placed in the competent hands of just the right doctors at just the right time. We took a deep breath and agreed to the surgery.

In pre-op we prayed, hugged, and said many "I love you's." We trembled as we watched this team of surgeons gather around our son as they rolled him into surgery. When those large steel doors closed behind them, our hearts plummeted.

With all that was at stake, it was hard to overcome the worries. I had to reach deep inside to find my mustard seed of faith. I had mountains to move!

Nearly six and a half hours later, all the procedures were complete. The surgeons came to talk with our family, and they were very pleased. It was a daunting surgery, but Gip had done remarkably well, all things considered. We were grateful for the "so far, so good" results, but anxious about what he still had to overcome. The doctors said we should be able to see Gip in about an hour.

By this time in our surgical "careers," we knew the routine. We did our usual postsurgery stretching and made another pass by the coffee pot to refortify ourselves for the next wait.

An hour and a half crept by, and we had not been approached by the recovery nurses to see Gip. We were getting a little anxious, so Richard asked the waiting-room receptionist if she had any updates on when we could see our son. She called the recovery room and then told him someone would be out to speak with us in a few minutes. Noticing a slightly odd expression on her face, Richard asked if everything was all right. She nodded, saying they would be out shortly.

We tried not to be alarmed. Prior experience had taught us that things could get hectic in the recovery area and cause delays. But after another half hour we became increasingly concerned.

I started getting a bad feeling in my gut. Then I began pacing. Okay, it was more like *racing*. I returned to the receptionist and asked her to contact someone to tell us what was going on. When she called the recovery room, she turned her chair around and covered her mouth as she spoke with them. I overheard her as she whispered, "The family is alarmed; you need to get someone out here."

I turned to Richard and said, "Something's wrong!"

Within minutes, a recovery nurse came to the waiting area and told us that Gip had suffered an intense seizure. She said they had him stabilized but that he'd been convulsing with such violence that they had called the neurosurgeon. They had run a CT scan and were waiting for results.

Another thirty minutes passed before we got any updated information. We were all about to pass out from anxiety and exhaustion by that time. Finally the neurosurgeon emerged and carefully explained what was happening and what the next steps were. He told us Gip was stable and the CT scan did not indicate any serious problems. He said that because of the seizure they would continue to monitor Gip in recovery until they felt he could be moved to ICU. The doctor assured us that he was not alarmed by this but rather cautiously concerned. His gentle manner comforted us greatly, but we were still battling fear of the unknown. We held hands and continued to pray for God's healing.

When we were finally able to see Gip, it was only for a few minutes. He looked ghastly—pale, swollen, and weak—with bandages on almost every area of his body. We hugged him as best we could, carefully avoiding contact with his many wounded body parts.

I desperately wanted to pick my child up and carry him out of there, to walk away from it all. Richard could see I was struggling to keep my composure. He gently took my hand and smiled as he leaned over and gave me a tender kiss on the cheek. We stood at Gip's bedside for a moment longer, but the nurses came in and asked us to leave so our child could rest.

Once Gip was stable enough to be moved to ICU, the caretaking that followed made our heads spin. Nurses were at his side 24/7. His head, stomach, and thigh were heavily bandaged from the procedures on each area. It was heartbreaking to see him in so much pain.

During the next few days, he developed several infections and high fevers. But they carefully managed those issues through medications, and amazingly Gip was discharged the following week.

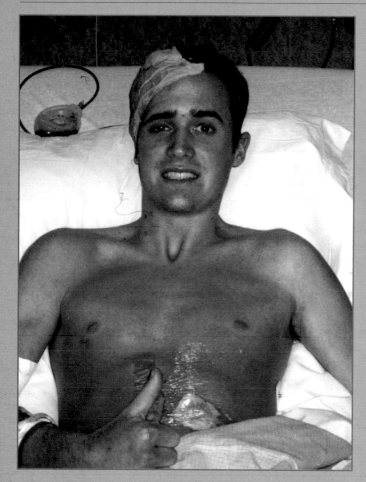

LEFT: Gip, just days after his miraculous split-skull surgery.

BELOW: Taylor, Beth, and Richard wearing the required protective gown, masks, and gloves in order to visit with Gip.

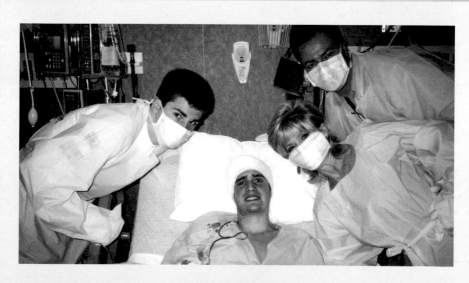

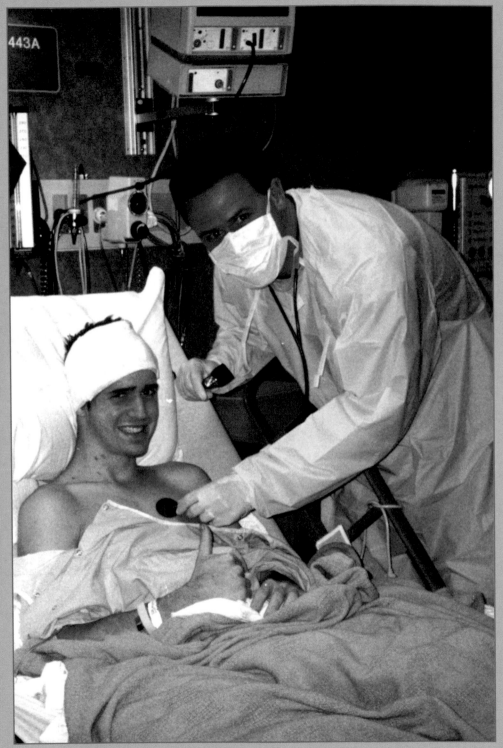

Coach Chuck changes his title to Doctor Chuck!

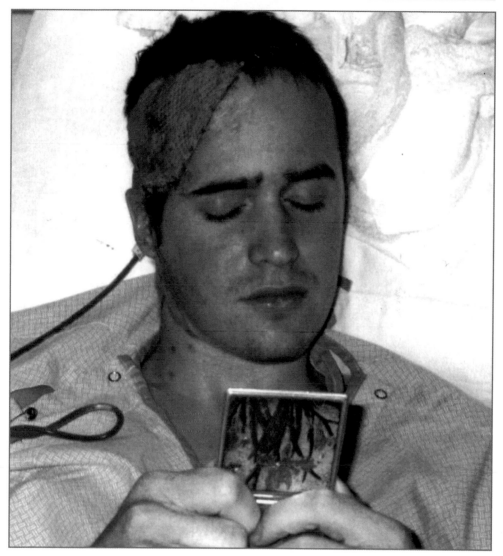
Gip looks in the mirror for the unveiling of his life-saving surgery

His surgical success has since become a topic at several medical seminars. The doctors were taking before-and-after photos throughout Gip's recovery. The procedure was quite a breakthrough, and they continued to note visual and medical updates on him. As for us, we were thankful God had led us to these incredible doctors whose brilliance and miraculous surgery brought hope and life back to our child's recovery, just in the nick of time.

By now, we had witnessed Gip conquer insurmountable odds. In many ways, he had survived the unsurvivable. With God, perhaps he *was* one in a million. The phrase isn't so bad when you think of it like that.

CHAPTER 31

Nurse Ratched

We were grateful to be home again. Unfortunately, we were also back to round-the-clock nursing care. Gip had a PICC line (peripherally inserted central catheter) in his arm, and through it we had to administer antibiotic fluids to him twice a day for ten weeks. We were also responsible for several dressing changes each day on his head, stomach, and thigh.

Administering an IV may not seem like a big deal, but the fear that came with this responsibility was overwhelming. It was much more than just monitoring medicinal doses; we had a list of side effects to watch out for. We often feared that our untrained eyes might miss something.

Our days and nights started running together. At times, I couldn't tell them apart. Being back on call to deal with serious 24/7 nursing duties was just about the last straw. I had alarms set all over the house in fear I might not wake up to give Gip his next treatment, his next pill, or even his next meal.

I typed up a list of Gip's schedules: medications, bandage changes, and therapies. I put copies in every room so that no matter where we might be, I would know what needed to be done and when. And God forbid, if anything happened to me, someone else would know what to do. I tried not to think of that *God forbid* part, but I feared it often, as I was so run down and weak myself.

Sometimes we spent days without ever leaving Gip's bedroom. As he would fall asleep, so would I. When he woke, I got up. In some ways it reminded me of when he was a newborn, except those days were also filled with resounding joy. Suffice it to say, these days were not.

On days when Gip felt up to it, Richard and Taylor helped bring him, his wheelchair, his IV pole, and other medical apparatus downstairs for a much-needed change of scenery. We'd eat, drink, sleep, and take meds in the family room for weeks at a time. When Richard came home at night, he would help Gip with his bath. But with so many tubes, wires, and open wounds all over his body, it was not an easy task and sometimes more trouble than it was worth.

Waking Gip night after night to check his vitals, change his bandages, and hook him up to the IV had grown old fast . . . for both of us. Patience was running thin, and there were days when tempers were flaring. Gip was tired of me constantly waking him up, and I was snapping back, saying that it had to be done.

My friend Joy came by several times when she knew we needed someone to break the tension of this intense nursing care. She was well-named, as *joy* is exactly what she brought to us. We might have been stressed and snapping at each other all the rest of the day, but when Joy was around, we were all smiles. So Gip began calling her "Nurse Feel Good."

As much as that name tickled us all, it brought to the surface a little title that Gip had for his *other* nurse—me. As he thanked Nurse Feel Good for stopping by, I asked Gip in jest what *my* nurse name was. Gip looked at Joy and winked as he said, "Nurse Ratched!"—referring to the monstrous nurse from the movie *One Flew Over the Cuckoo's Nest*. This was not exactly a title I'd hoped to acquire!

After ten weeks, Gip was finally released from the infectious-disease doctors, and we were able to discontinue his IV antibiotics. We were all anxious to take that chore off our plates. We then worked hard to get back to our less medical roles of caretaking . . . and life.

I was doing my best to shed my new title. So one day I decided to put on a tiara, a gift I'd received months earlier from my friend Bev, who'd had a "Mother of the Year" nameplate engraved and attached to the front of the headpiece. Of course, Gip asked me why I was wearing such a thing.

I immediately informed him that the tiara was my crown for having just been named Mother of the Year.

"By who?" he asked.

"By *me!*" I replied.

He smiled, nodded, and hugged me as he said, "You've earned it, Mom. It looks great on you!"

I wore it all day long. I even danced around the room a few times with self-admiration! It helped bring back the humor that had been absent in our lives for a while.

CHAPTER 32

Help From Beyond

We were grateful for every card or letter we received, and read many of them more than once. It was comforting to know that so many people were praying for our child, for our family, at such a time of need. Today we have a huge chest, kept in Gip's bedroom, filled with thousands of get-well cards.

Why did so many people reach out to us? I honestly don't have an answer to that question. Chuck's prayer chain had a lot to do with spreading the news, but the kindness in people's hearts took over beyond that. We didn't earn this outpouring of love and support. No one can do that. We're just an ordinary little family from an ordinary little suburb, living an ordinary little life. But there's nothing ordinary about what we've experienced. We've seen extraordinary acts of kindness and compassion.

When Gip was in the hospital, we received many gifts—prayer blankets, holy water, anointed oils, crosses, angel pendants, and more. Taffy, my life-long best friend, sent items each week that had been made especially for Gip and prayed over by her church. As he lay in his hospital bed in unbearable pain and anxiety, Richard and I often stood on either side and gently placed our hands and these gifts over every aching part of his body. We kept Gip covered in prayer *and* prayer blankets at all times. We pinned the crosses to his sheets, hung the angel pendants over his bed, and dabbed his body with the anointed oils and blessed holy water. We did anything we could think of that might help. I'm sure there are still some nurses who wonder about us and our spiritual activities, but I would've danced on the ceiling if someone told me it would help my child!

Another gift came in the form of our neighbors, Dr. Jim Majors and his wife, Marcy. Jim is a general surgeon, and Marcy is a neurological ICU nurse. Jim often stopped by after work to check on Gip. He knew we were overwhelmed by all the healthcare needs that were now ours to tend to, and he kindly and patiently addressed our concerns. Marcy was wonderful as well. It was comforting to know such medical expertise was so close by.

One time in particular Marcy truly came to our rescue. It was my regular routine to check on Gip several times throughout the night, and this night had been no different. But when I walked in his room that next morning, there was blood all over his arm, chest, and sheets.

I rushed to his side and began calling his name. He didn't answer. I immediately checked his pulse—something no mother should ever have to do! I could barely feel his heartbeat. His skin was clammy, and he wasn't responding. I ran to the phone and called 911. It was actually *busy!* I flew down the stairs, ran out the front door, and rushed across the street to Marcy's home.

I banged on the door and continuously pressed the doorbell, all the while frantically screaming her name. Marcy was upstairs bathing her baby and didn't hear my calls at first. Finally she came soaking-wet to the door, carrying her naked, soap-covered son in her arms. She knew by the look on my face there was an immediate need.

It was freezing cold outside. Even though we rarely get snow in our area, we had several inches on the ground that day. But that didn't stop us from dashing half-dressed across our snow-covered cul-de-sac, with Marcy's baby protected by nothing more than a little hand towel. As we raced to my house, I gasped for breath and tried to explain what was going on with Gip.

We flew into the house and rushed upstairs. I could hear Gip faintly calling my name. He must have been beginning to wake up and was clearly frightened by the sight of all the blood. When we got to his room, he was lying there with a terrified look on his face. I did my best to reassure him that he was all right, but I'm sure my expression of fear conflicted with my words of comfort. Marcy reassured Gip that he was okay as she handed her child to me and began to work her medical magic.

I don't recall exactly what she did, but she stopped the bleeding that was coming from Gip's IV PICC line, and within minutes the color in Gip's face—and mine—returned. Once the immediate crisis was over, Marcy reached over and hugged me as I sank into her angelic arms.

CHAPTER 33

Houdini

When Gip first came home from the hospital, he still required the use of a wheelchair. As he grew a little stronger, he began using a walker. As time went on, he became more and more mobile and was pretty much walking unaided. It was a tremendous step in his physical and emotional recovery.

But not all concerns were remedied by his return to walking. Gip was still prone to seizures, and we were told to be on full alert for them at all times. We had to be sure he didn't have a seizure that could cause him to fall and possibly injure his head again. I was almost paralyzed with fear about this. I found myself staring at him almost every waking minute.

Gip grew very weary of me constantly asking him if he felt all right, was he dizzy or light-headed, did he feel odd in any way. After a stretch of my continual drilling, he would finally say that he wanted to go to bed. Of course even that prompted more health questions as I wondered why he was tired and what had made him sleepy all of a sudden.

Looking back, it's a wonder he didn't string me up by my toes! But somehow we found a happy medium where we could both have some peace in our day. Gip promised to give me a heads-up if he felt strange in any way, and I promised not to ask more than twice a day. We shook on it and laughed as we tried to get on with our "new normal" lives.

But there was yet another great concern. With all the surgeries Gip had undergone, his scalp was covered with scars. Many were deep and came with severed nerve endings that were trying to heal and grow back together. The body is a natural healer, if let be. But that was not easy for Gip.

He felt an irresistible urge to scratch. The doctors explained this overwhelming itching sensation to be much like having your head on fire. They said it was a million times worse than any itch most people ever experience. Since scratching is a natural, impulsive response to an itch, the doctors were concerned. They needed to be certain Gip did not damage his fragile skin, causing his wound to reopen.

Their concerns were magnified over what damage might occur at night, when Gip had no consciousness to refrain from scratching. It was a scary situation for us all. Finally, a decision was made to put our son in a straitjacket. Yes, a straitjacket.

It was incredibly difficult for Gip *and* us to understand the need for this. But as Gip slept, he inadvertently clawed at his head because of the horrendous itching. Keeping his arms strapped to his body was the only solution to prevent more infections, more wound openings, and more surgeries. It was the lesser of the two evils, I guess. But it tore out hearts out to do it.

The first few weeks at home, I was too scared to leave Gip's side through the night, so I slept in a bed just beside his. As time went on, he seemed to be sleeping well through the night, so I graduated to sleeping in the hallway.

I did this to give Gip a sense of privacy. The doctors and psychologists told us how important privacy was in improving a patient's morale. So I was very conscientious about that. We set up a small cot with blankets and a pillow just outside Gip's room, and that became my bed for the next month.

Once I felt comfortable leaving this post, I moved downstairs to our master bedroom, which allowed both of us to get some much-needed rest in our separate quarters. A friend loaned us her baby monitor, with a video monitor as well as an audio one. Sometimes the video monitor sent out light flashes that woke us in the middle of the night. So as time went on and our concerns lessened, we turned off the video and began using only the audio.

Weeks later, in the morning's wee hours, I was awakened by the sound of a flushing toilet. My first thought was that it must have been Taylor. Gip was strapped into his bed in a straitjacket, so it couldn't possibly have been him.

Nevertheless, I flew upstairs to check it out. As I reached the top step, I glanced in Taylor's room and saw that he was sound asleep. Confused, I quickly stepped across the hall to check on Gip. I quietly peeked through the crack of his bedroom door.

Much to my surprise, I saw Gip very nonchalantly walking to his bed. Stunned, I watched him as he climbed in between the sheets and carefully began the tedious process of restrapping himself into his straitjacket. I couldn't believe my eyes. All this time we thought he was safely strapped in, safe from falling if he had a seizure and unable to scratch if he had an itch. But our resident Houdini had us all fooled.

Night after night, he lay there patiently allowing us to strap him in. As we tearfully apologized each time for having to do such a thing, Gip would smile and tell us he understood why we had to do it and that he didn't mind. Well, of course he didn't mind; he knew he wasn't really trapped!

Uncertain how to handle things at the moment, I did not go into Gip's room that night. I let him think his cover had not been blown. I watched him through the door crack for a little longer as he comfortably settled into his strappings. Since it was clear he was all right and no damage had been done, I lay down in the hallway just outside his room and fell asleep.

I must admit I was amused by all this. This was so Gip. Even though he had been through a lot of changes, Gip still had an athlete's mindset of "where there's a will, there's a way." He had figured out how to maneuver his legs up and down, moving the jacket's body flap up close to his chin, putting him in a position where he could then begin gnawing on the knots we'd tied to each strap around his shoulders. Once those straps were loose, he used his teeth to pull out each knot around his arms and wrists. And there he lay, free as a bird, happy as a clam. He was able to get up whenever and for whatever he wanted, all night long.

Keenly aware of my nightly nurse routine, Gip knew exactly when I made my last round to check on my patient. As I said good night and checked on his straps, he must've had a sheepish grin on his face that I was unaware of. Clearly he was waiting until I was done for the night, so he could break loose.

The following morning as I lay in the hallway, I woke up to find that Taylor had propped a pillow under my head and placed a blanket over me. Knowing of my ongoing aching neck, he carefully and quietly took care of his mama. I still tear up thinking about how many things Taylor did that perhaps went unnoticed.

As I quietly got up from the hall floor, I peeked into Gip's room and saw that he was still fast asleep. I waited until the usual morning medicine hour and walked in asking him, "So, Houdini, how was your night?" He looked at me with a puzzled look, but before he could say anything, I started laughing.

"Am I busted?" he asked.

"You are so busted!" I replied, and began my "mama safety lecture." After that we both resumed our belly laughing. I'm amused now just thinking of how he lay there each morning, pretending he needed me to undo his straps so he could get out of bed for the day.

By God's grace, nothing bad happened. Gip did not have a seizure or fall out of the bed, and fortunately he never tore out stitches with a scratching attack. Because no harm was done, we were able to laugh at his Houdini antics.

CHAPTER 34

Back to Life

Eye of the Beholder

Ten weeks after Gip's surgery, his doctors finally released him from medical restrictions. This allowed him to begin outpatient therapy. It had been seven months since his accident, and he was anxious to get back on the road to recovery. He spent about three months at Pathways, Shepherd Center's outpatient facility. When he graduated, we all but bought him *and me* a cap and gown!

As we began to move outside the hospital and rehab arenas, we had to adjust to more than just the changes we could see. We had to adjust to the changes other people could see.

Gip was so good at not allowing others to feel sorry for him that even I didn't feel it . . . most of the time. I guess I didn't see it either. In our eyes, Gip looked fantastic. He had come a long, long way from that eerie sight the night of his accident. So to us, he looked amazing—"divinely recreated," one might say.

But to others, it was quite a shock to see how bone-thin he'd become, how pale he was, and how slowly he moved. Gip tired easily, and his physical demeanor showed it. He also had quite a few scars on his face, his head, and all over his body. His eyes were deeply sunken from the severity of the trauma, and he appeared gray and gaunt due to the tremendous lack of sleep.

His head, still severely swollen, had to remain wrapped in bandages. All these changes made some people very uncomfortable. At times, they even stared with disbelief. But Gip's endearing spirit always responded with a smile, and that usually put them at ease.

We also had to adjust to the new label that had been given to our son. Each time we went to a medical facility or doctor's office, they listed him as "disabled," a victim of TBI. I certainly wasn't bothered by the term "disabled," and I was well aware that our son had a traumatic brain injury. But the look was sometimes tough to handle. You know the one—that "I'm so sorry" look.

By this time, Gip had undergone numerous surgeries and spent many months in intensive therapies trying to recover from his injury, his disability. He had come a long way. I found myself confused as to why others were seeing him as *dis*-abled, instead of gloriously *abled*, as we saw him. I felt they needed to take a closer look and see all the abilities our child had worked so hard to achieve, not focus on his disabilities.

But I've since learned to embrace this label—and any other label given to our child—with all my heart. Every time someone puts Gip in the "disabled" category, it gives him an opportunity to share what he's learned about being disabled. It's been a gift to watch him encourage others to see themselves as he sees himself: disabled in some ways but, through God, very able in others.

I am thankful for all this has taught me and my family. It has provided each of us with an avenue to help others in ways we never could have before. It's hard to imagine that so much good could come from so much tragedy. Yet it has.

It's all in the eye of the beholder.

Take Me Out to the Ball Game

Nearly eight months after Gip's accident, he was invited to throw out the first pitch for the varsity baseball team's season opener at his alma mater, Collins Hill High School. Having played on the team, Gip had several ex-coaches who became "charter members" of his prayer team. They were thrilled to have Gip back on the diamond.

The bleachers were packed with baseball fans and Gip's friends. Other than for therapy sessions or medical appointments, this was his first time out of the house since his homecoming. Because for such a long time he had not been allowed to have visitors, many had not seen Gip since his accident. There was quite a crowd building in the stands.

Chuck was the master of ceremonies. He stood in the press box and began to say a few words about Gip, highlighting his high school baseball career, his accident, and God's miracle in his life. Then Chuck introduced Gip, and the crowd went wild.

"And here he is!" Chuck announced. With that, Richard and I turned to help Gip walk out on the field, but he was gone. He'd been standing at our side, and all of a sudden he had disappeared. Richard and I began frantically searching for him. Chuck said a few more words and reintroduced Gip. Again, nothing. "Where is he?" Chuck asked over the loudspeaker.

Richard found Gip in the batting cages behind the baseball field. He was warming up his throwing arm, getting ready for his pitching debut. This didn't really surprise Richard. He gave Gip the nod of "one more pitch" and then said, "It's game time buddy, let's go." They walked back to the baseball field.

Chuck got a big kick out of Gip's competitive spirit. He laughed as he told the crowd that Gip was practicing his pitch so he could "bring it" that day. Once again, Chuck introduced Gip, and once again the crowd stood and cheered for our son.

Ghastly pale, barely weighing a hundred pounds, with a feeding tube plugged into his stomach, an IV PICC line inserted in his upper left arm, and a damaged sense of balance, Gip proudly walked onto his alma mater's baseball field.

At that time Gip was still very weak. We weren't sure if he was physically able to throw out a pitch, especially from such a distance—from the pitcher's mound all the way to the catcher. So the coach offered to let him throw the ball from a few feet away. But, of course, Gip would have nothing to do with that. He was a ballplayer; he was there to pitch regulation baseball, from the mound.

The coach handed him the ball, shook his hand, and wished him luck. As Gip turned around, his smile lit up the stadium. Then a sudden hush fell upon the crowd. It got so quiet you could've heard a pin drop. Chills traveled up and down our spines as our hearts pounded in our chests.

Chuck, in his humorous fashion, lightened the mood by reminding the crowd that Gip's baseball position had been at shortstop, not pitcher. He jokingly warned everyone to protect themselves from a possible wild pitch.

Creatively, Chuck described each detail of Gip's windup and pitch. "He's on the pitcher's mound, folks." The crowd began cheering. Chuck continued, "and now for the strategical placement of his toe on the rubber." He paused for a moment and said, "Here comes the lean forward and the all-important signal from the catcher."

After a quick breath, Chuck's volume increased as he announced, "Gip's got his game face on, ladies and gentlemen, so watch out." And just a split second later, Chuck blurted out, "There goes the wind-up. And now . . . the pitch!"

You could feel the earth move as the entire stadium seemed take a deep breath together. Then, with overwhelming joy, Chuck screamed out, "It paints the outside right corner, folks. It's a strrrrrrike!"

By this time, everyone was on their feet and applauding. We all cheered as if Gip had just won the World Series with his pitch. Of course, *we* felt Gip had won something far greater than that in his personal battle.

The team won the game that day, and newspaper reporters quoted the head coach, Paul Pierce, as saying, "The greatest victory is that we won one for the Gipper."

TOP: Gip walks to the pitcher's mound to throw out the first pitch of the season for his alma mater, Collins Hill High School. His former baseball coach, Paul Pierce, wishes him good luck. **MIDDLE:** Gip leans in to read the catcher's pitch signal. **BOTTOM:** Gip throws the pitch . . . and it's a strike!

Knucksie

It seemed quite timely that the day after Gip threw out the first pitch at his high school alma mater's baseball game, he was treated to lunch by the legendary Atlanta Braves pitcher and 1997 Hall of Famer, Phil Niekro. Because of his phenomenal knuckleball pitch, the press had fondly nicknamed him "Knucksie."

When Gip was in high school, he was blessed to have played a few seasons of American Legion baseball. One of his team's honorary coaches was Phil Niekro. Mr. Niekro is not only a renowned baseball player; he is a great man as well. Everyone was in awe of meeting him and having the honor of him coaching our sons.

He's so down to earth that he treated *us* like celebrities. It was quite a gift for Gip and his teammates to have such a wonderful, talented gentleman as part of their coaching staff. The boys love him, and so do we. Mr. Niekro is quite personable and insists that we call him by his first name; so hereafter, it's Phil.

After Gip's accident, Phil called and sent cards to Gip, letting us know that he and his family were lifting Gip in prayer. One time when he came to visit Gip at the hospital, Gip had taken quite a bad turn and was not expected to make it through the night. At the time, we did not realize that Phil was on his way to see Gip, and unfortunately we had just walked down to the hospital chapel when he arrived.

When we returned, the nurse told us that Gip had had a visitor while we were gone. She said he left a gift. We walked into Gip's ICU cubicle and saw a baseball cap sitting on the table next to his bed. Richard picked up the official Georgia Sports Hall of Fame baseball cap and read the handwritten note out loud: "To Gip. You are *my* Hall of Famer. Your Friend, Phil Niekro."

Coach Niekro's signed baseball hat, a gift for Gip at the hospital.

I have been inspired by Gip's faith, determination, and drive.
—*Phil Niekro, Hall-of-Fame baseball pitcher for the Atlanta Braves*

Mere words just can't describe how much that meant to us. We can only imagine what Phil must have felt when he saw Gip in such critical condition. We were sorry we had missed Phil's visit, but his gift and heartfelt message lifted our spirits immeasurably.

The ball cap, along with a signed photo from Knucksie's days with the Atlanta Braves, hangs in Gip's room today as one of his prized possessions. Phil will forever hold a special place in Gip's heart . . . and ours.

Gip with American Legion coaches Phil Niekro and
Earl Corder, celebrating Gip's recovery.

Gip and Beth
with Phil Niekro,
going to lunch
to celebrate
Gip's recovery.

Meet the Gipper

Shortly after Gip's pitching debut, the chaos in our lives was settling down a bit. As we began processing all we'd been through, we were desperately trying to find a way to express our gratitude for the many kindnesses shown to our family. It had been about eight months since Gip's accident, and we couldn't imagine how we could possibly thank everyone.

In yet another effort to help our family, Chuck set up a gathering of Gip's prayer warriors—a place where we could express our appreciation and where those who hadn't known Gip before his accident could finally meet the young man they had so fervently prayed for. Chuck and another Young Life angel, Lauri, worked for several weeks putting together a "Meet the Gipper" night at a local church.

We were nervous about handling our emotions at such an event. This was not something we could've prepared ourselves for. When Chuck saw the anxiety on my face, he hugged me and said, "Don't worry. God's got this! All you have to do is show up."

Coach Chuck and the Gayle family before the
Meet the Gipper celebration.

Well, we showed up. And we were overwhelmed at the turnout of more than eight hundred people at this gathering.

Once again, Chuck was the master of ceremonies. He started the night by introducing Gip and our family. We walked up on the altar. Everyone stood and clapped. It seemed to last an uncomfortably long time.

We were like fish out of water, uncertain what to say or how to act. Our eyes began to fill with tears as we looked around the room in awe of what surrounded us. It was awkward, but beautiful. I can remember turning toward Richard and whispering, "Is this really happening?" After all we'd been through, it was quite surreal.

Chuck opened the evening with a prayer, thanking God for His amazing miracle in Gip's life. Then Scott, Gip's other Young Life mentor, led us in song. He selected one of Gip's favorites: "I Can Only Imagine" by Mercy Me. The lyrics are about what it will be like when we get to Heaven, something we can only imagine. By the time that song ended, there wasn't a dry eye in the house.

Scott then spoke for a while about what this experience meant to him. He had our hearts wrapped around his every word as he shared how he marveled at God's grace in Gip's survival and recovery. Then came Scott's humorous side. He told the story of going to Savannah shortly after finding out his wife, Emily, was pregnant with their first child. Scott had encouraged Gip to work extra hard with the incentive that he might name their baby "Gip."

As Scott spoke, Emily was sitting in the front pew, expected to deliver at any moment. Barely able to move, she busted out laughing at the baby name story. She shouted, "It might be a girl, you know."

Gip with Scott and Emily Spears, parents of Gip's namesake.

I stood up and shouted back, "Then we'll call her Gipette!" (Four days later, they had a baby boy and named him Sawyer. But *we* call him "Little Gip"!)

Next, Chuck took the microphone and slowly walked to the altar. His tense body language showed he was struggling to keep it together. The audience's mood quickly changed. He began to speak but stopped suddenly. He looked over at his wife, Julie, and she gave him a smile of encouragement. He smiled back at her and then looked up, as if to get help from above.

He held the mike at his side, but we heard him as he whispered, "Lord, help me do this." As tears filled his eyes, he took another minute to regroup. Gradually he began to talk about what he called "the most amazing God-filled experience he'd ever had."

As Chuck spoke, his voice cracked with emotion several times. He paused, resting the mike against his chest trying to gather his composure. He reminisced about his friendship with Gip and how they both grew in their faith through this experience. He was visibly moved as he reviewed what we had been through—what he had been through with us. He was overwhelmed that we had come to this glorious day.

He thanked everyone for their prayers and told them of the power it brought to our family. He told of Gip's strong will and determination to get better and how the strength of God got him through each challenge.

Chuck choked up a bit and then stated emphatically, "I believe we've witnessed a miracle here!" He went on to say, "Do *not* forget this moment in your lives, for God has brought you here for a reason." He finished up by saying, "Let this miracle bless you today. And let it continue to bless you for the rest of your lives."

The power with which Chuck spoke was beyond anything I've ever heard, and I do believe that everyone there will remember that moment and will remember witnessing one of God's miracles.

I have always believed that God can do all things, but having experienced this miracle up close and personal has given me greater faith and a story to share with others. Our families' involvement with Gip and this miracle has been a special gift and blessing in our lives. As difficult and touch and go as it was, we were privileged to witness the extraordinary courage and faith of the Gayle family. My children have a story of hope to share and to stand on for the rest of their lives.

—Julie Scott, wife of Gip's coach, Chuck Scott

Then Chuck introduced Gip. Everyone stood and began clapping and cheering. Gip was nervous. Being front and center has never been his forte, so it was not easy for him to be on stage with a mike in his hand. Knowing this, Chuck had prepared a little humorous question-and-answer session between them. It was clever and corny, and we all enjoyed seeing these two buddies perform.

When they finished, Gip stood to say a few words of thanks. It got very quiet, as we were all anxious to hear him speak. He thanked everyone for their prayers. He then expressed his gratitude to God for giving him the strength to keep fighting. He paused for a moment as he turned to Chuck. They shared an emotional hug as Gip publicly thanked Chuck for always being there for him. He called him his hero and said that he couldn't have recovered without him. When Gip turned around, he gave a quick shout-out to his fraternity brothers, and they stood and cheered.

Gip and Chuck sharing Gip's story with more than 800 of Gip's prayer warriors.

I cannot describe what our family felt at that moment. It was hard to imagine that we almost lost our child just months earlier.

Chuck then handed the microphone to Taylor. Once again we were bursting at the seams with pride when our precious baby—a baby no lon-ger—stood in front of more than eight hundred people and said his own thank you's.

Taylor thanked everyone who prayed for his brother. He thanked our friends and their families for taking care of him, for feeding him, for taking him to school, for supporting him at his games, and so on. He thanked his friends for coming to Savannah and for always being there for him.

He paused for a moment as he looked over at the Isbill family . . . his second family. Taylor thanked them for opening their home and hearts to him. He said he had never felt like he was a burden or an outsider, that they treated him like he was one of their own. He told them how grateful he felt to know and love such an amazing family.

He then began clapping for the Isbills. Soon everyone joined in the applause for this precious family.

Richard was next. He took the mike, walked up to the podium, and stood there for a moment—a long moment. He then began to pour his heart out.

He started by saying, "On September 6, 2003, my life changed forever, and so did the lives of my family." Tears were already flowing, but somehow he managed to go on. He looked up and said, "There were times when I didn't think we'd make it. But we did. With your help and the power of your prayers, we got through this nightmare."

Richard thanked Chuck and Lauri for putting the "Meet the Gipper" night together, giving us a chance to thank everyone. He said he was honored that so many people had come to meet our son. He then looked down, grabbed both sides of the podium, and stood a little taller as he reminded everyone of what that night was *really* about—celebrating God's miracle. Everyone clapped in agreement.

Richard paused, took a sip of water and continued, "As I look around this room tonight I see the face of Jesus. I've seen Him in old friends, I've seen Him in new friends, and I see Him right now in some of you whom I've yet to meet." He looked down for a moment and then held his head high as he said loudly, "Thank you, prayer warriors, for saving our lives!"

As Richard stood there with his heart overflowing, he humbly thanked everyone who helped him take care of his family. He expressed his gratitude like no one else could. He was the father, the head of the house that crumbled, and family, friends, and strangers had graciously stepped up to fill his role whenever and wherever it was needed. Again, not a dry eye in the house.

Then it was my turn. I have little memory of what I said, as I was pretty much numb the whole time. I do remember making a few jokes in the beginning. It seemed necessary to lighten the mood after Richard's heartfelt talk.

Suddenly, I could feel the emotions stirring deep within me. Tears were rushing to the surface; the floodgates were about to open. I took a step back, turned my head, and looked at Richard, who was sitting just behind the podium. My body was screaming SOS!

Richard quickly sat up in his chair, smiled at me, and gave me the nod. You know the one—that "you can do it" nod. I took a deep breath and turned back around. As I looked across the room, I saw many familiar faces. All I could think was, "How do I even *begin* to thank them?"

I more or less fumbled my way through my first few words. But then I looked up and simply said, "Not long ago our lives were shattered, and I didn't think we'd ever be put back together again. But you held us together. I don't know how we'll ever be able to thank you for that."

I went on to thank Chuck for all that he meant to us. I also thanked his beautiful wife, Julie. For we know that in order for Chuck to have done all he did for us, he had to have an amazing wife at home taking care of *their* family, so he could help take care of ours.

Hanging behind me was a picture Richard had painted as a memento of our experience. It's a scene of a fountain just outside the Savannah hospital where Gip spent the first month after his accident.

Richard's painting "Rays of Hope," showing the Savannah hospital fountain where Beth and Richard spent many hours praying for healing.

Many times, Richard and I had stared at this fountain as we prayed for healing. The sun's rays seemed to glisten as they danced on the falling water. It was as if the rays were coming directly from Heaven. So we began calling them our "Rays of Hope."

I explained the significance of Richard's painting and then read our family thank-you poem. It was something I'd written in an effort to capture that moment in time. It was important to our family to express our gratitude, but we mainly wanted to keep God's glory in all this alive—forever!

At the evening's end, we handed out note cards with Richard's painting of our "Rays of Hope" on one side and our family thank-you poem on the other. Here 'tis!

Rays of Hope

When you look at this picture and think of our story
Remember the power of prayer and all of God's glory
Keep faith in your lives and hope in your hearts
And remember this miracle in which you took part

For when we all stopped and fell to our knees
God's power emerged and He answered our pleas
For He loves us so much and He truly is listening
Just look around you—you can see God is glistening

How can we ever thank you for your kindness and love
Why you're God's precious angels sent to us from above
You've touched our lives in so many ways
You've "been there" for us through some really tough days

We've seen the Face of Jesus in you each day
Blessed with you by our side, we have found the way
The Way, The Truth, and The Life
Together we've lived it through triumph and strife

Mere words can't express how you've lifted us
And now it's time for *us* to make the fuss
It's time that we give *you* your due praise
For your unending generosity and loving ways

So, thank you, dear friends, for holding us so tight
Thank you for caring and loving us just right
Thank you for all of your prayers that took flight
God bless you for sharing in Gip's miracle of might!

Chapter 35

His Favorite Comedian

O n the day of Gip's accident, he was wearing a camouflage ball cap autographed by the famous comedian Jeff Foxworthy. Jeff is a huge Young Life supporter and has donated many signed items to the organization. When Gip was a high school senior, he had won a YL contest, and the prize was that autographed cap. It became Gip's favorite hat. He even called it his lucky hat! Hmmm . . .

When Gip was shot, the birdshot from the gun went right through the middle of Jeff's signature—between *Jeff* and *Foxworthy*—pretty much destroying the cap.

Gip was clearly bummed about the loss of his favorite hat. Knowing that, Chuck once again swung into action. This time was a little different, though. He was embarking on what seemed an impossible mission, because Chuck did not know Jeff Foxworthy. But that didn't stop him from trying to track him down.

The Foxworthy autographed ball cap Gip was wearing when he was shot.

Jeff lives in Georgia, in the Atlanta area, so Chuck was determined to find him somehow in hopes of getting another signed hat for Gip. Chuck made numerous phone calls throughout the day attempting to find somebody who could reach Jeff, but to no avail.

Then, that very night, as Chuck was at his son's basketball practice, in walked none other than Jeff Foxworthy. Jeff was there to watch his daughter's basketball practice. He sat on the parents' bleachers only a few seats away from Chuck. At that point, Chuck knew this was no accident—divine intervention was in play.

Chuck walked over to Jeff, asking forgiveness for disturbing his private time with his family, and told him he had "quite a God moment to share with him." Because of Jeff's Christian heart and his compassion toward others, he responded with curiosity. As Chuck began to tell Jeff about Gip's accident and amazing recovery, Jeff leaned in with more interest. Chuck told Jeff about Gip's favorite Foxworthy-autographed hat being destroyed in the accident and asked if he could get another signed hat. Jeff quickly responded, saying, "I'll get him a whole box of hats!" He also said he'd like to meet him one day. They exchanged contact information and agreed to set up a time for Jeff to meet Gip.

When Jeff got home that night, he told his wife, Gregg, about this amazing survival story of a young man shot in the head in a hunting accident. Gregg immediately spoke up, saying, "Are you talking about Gip Gayle?" Taken by surprise, Jeff asked how she knew who he was. Gregg explained that her ladies' Bible study group had received an email prayer request about this young man and had added him to its prayer list. Goose bumps!

Within a week, Jeff and Gregg were at our home meeting Gip and our family. Of course Chuck was with us to enjoy this special moment. It was an amazing night. Jeff and Gip hit it off right away. Jeff brought not only a new signed ball cap but a whole box of hats, as promised. He also brought some Blue Collar comedy DVDs and Foxworthy hunting videos. He even autographed the bill on one of the new hats, adding a little note that reads: "Do not shoot this hat!"

Getting to know Beth Gayle, and coming alongside her for a part of her journey through this crisis, has been one of the most significant times of my life. I have cried with Beth, laughed (a lot) with Beth, and been totally awed and inspired by the depth of her faith and the breadth of her love. She is special!

—Gregg Foxworthy, wife of comedian Jeff Foxworthy

Jeff brings Gip a whole box of hats and other autographed items.

Gip shows Jeff Foxworthy where the shot went between "Jeff" and "Foxworthy."

Gip and Taylor with Jeff Foxworthy.

Gip and family, along with Chuck, Jeff Foxworthy, and Jeff's wife, Gregg.

Gip was thrilled to be sitting in our living room visiting his favorite comedian. Jeff had us laughing like we hadn't laughed in a long time. Meeting him and his precious wife brought a unique healing to our family that night.

Thanks to Chuck, Gip got a new Foxworthy-autographed hat and a lifetime memory of what kindness and humor are all about.

Gip's new hat, which reads, "Do not shoot this hat!"

You Might Be a Redneck If . . .

While Jeff and Gregg were visiting, our dog was scratching at the back door begging to come inside. Jeff saw Yeller and commented on how awesome it must have been for Gip to see his dog after such a long time away. Gip smiled sheepishly and told Jeff she was the first thing he asked about when he came out of his coma. Jeff was taken aback as Gip explained that when he woke up, he saw all of his family at his bedside and wondered who was tending to his dog. So the first thing he said was "How's Yeller?"

Gip introduces Yeller to Jeff.

Jeff busted out laughing and said, "Gip, I do believe I found another redneck joke for my act!" He paused for a moment as if to get into character for his new joke and said, "If your first words coming out of a coma are 'how's my dog,' you might be a redneck." We laughed so hard it hurt!

Jeff said he would put that joke in his upcoming Redneck Calendar. He said he was a dog lover, too, and that this story touched his heart so much it will forever be in his Redneck Hall of Fame jokes.

Then Jeff asked for the date of Gip's accident, saying he would put the joke on that calendar day. Gip told him September 6. Jeff's jaw dropped as he looked over at his wife, Gregg, and they both shook their heads in disbelief. Unsure what they were stunned about, Gip asked what was wrong.

Jeff slowly replied, "Gip, that's my birthday." More goose bumps!

The calendar page Jeff dedicated to Gip.

CHAPTER 36

Adjusting

Gip with Yeller on the one-year anniversary of God's miracle!

During months nine through twelve of Gip's recovery, we were trying to make adjustments for what Gip could and could not do. He had finished his inpatient rehabilitation, graduated from his outpatient therapies, and was now at home continuing to recover. He had come a long, long way. But there was still much more to recover from.

The brain is an amazing instrument and can heal in astonishing ways. But even with miracles helping along the way, it takes time for that to happen and for patients to return to being themselves physically, mentally, and emotionally.

To people seeing Gip home from the hospital—finished with his therapies, more or less surgically repaired, and even throwing out baseballs at high school season openers—he appeared healed. In many ways, he was. But there were still so many unanswered questions about Gip's future.

Each of us was determined to help him continue the fight to get his life back. But we weren't exactly sure what Gip's life was anymore. Clearly, he was on a different path now after such an accident. We all were. We were struggling to figure out what the next step should be, and answers did not come easily. We seemed to be at a bit of a standstill.

Now that Gip was finished with his official therapies, he was anxious to get back to college. But he was nowhere near ready. We knew it, and he knew it. It was tough to deal with that daily despair.

We reached out for sound advice from Gip's therapists. They were always very encouraging but advised us not to move too far, too fast. It was critical that we set Gip up for success, not failure. That's often a fine line. But Gip was determined to return to school, and he worked diligently the next several months to achieve that goal. At summer's end, we revisited his therapists for further evaluation. They suggested he take one or two college courses at first to see how he handled the workload.

To be admitted to college, Gip was required to pass a math entrance exam. Prior to his accident, his math skills had been fairly strong. But all things were in question now. Besides the obvious concern of his brain injury, Gip had been out of school for almost a year by that time. And he certainly hadn't been brushing up on his math skills. He was going to need some one-on-one tutoring.

Sue Schafer, a friend who is also a math teacher at our local high school, kindly offered to help Gip relearn some of the skills required to pass his assessment. It was not an easy task, but Sue's patience and determination to help Gip reach his goal were evident from the start. Gip was clearly the teacher's pet. She gave her undivided attention to him evenings and weekends for several weeks as he struggled to regain the math skills he'd once mastered.

When they both felt he was ready, we scheduled his exam. Days later, Gip courageously walked through those big heavy doors at the college admissions office and walked down to the testing room. I waited in the lobby as my child worked his way through what seemed one of the more important exams of his life.

Nearly a week passed before we got the results. To say we were on the edge of our seats would be an understatement. Thanks to Sue, Gip passed the test and was admitted to the local college. He immediately signed up for a couple of classes that following semester. By that time it was fall 2004, one full year since Gip's accident.

College semesters are about four months long, but it seemed like forever as we watched our son fight his way through learning, studying, and testing. We were all anxious to know if Gip could handle such a challenge.

After final exams, we had to wait another week before grades were post-ed. Hurray! Gip made B's in both of his classes. This was a huge boost to his morale, and ours. Chuck sent out an attaboy email, and we all celebrated online.

We realized Gip wasn't back at full steam yet, but this was an amazing feat. One baby step at a time, he was returning to the life he'd left behind.

CHAPTER 37

Back in the Saddle

Several weeks later, Jeff Foxworthy called Gip and invited him and Richard to go deer hunting on his private hunting farm. This was about a year and a half after Gip's accident and his first time returning to the hunting world since that fateful day.

Gip and Jeff give the thumbs-up
for Gip's return to hunting.

Getting back to hunting was a gift for Gip, but it was quite a struggle for me. Richard had been hesitant, too. But as a man, he was much more understanding of Gip's yearning. Hunters will tell you that once hunting is in your blood, you just can't get it out of your system, no matter what. It was tough to allow our son to hunt again. But Gip has told us many times, "I fought hard to survive. Now I want to live. For me, hunting is living!" As parents, we've had to accept and even embrace this.

As Richard and Gip set out to hunt with Jeff, they were joined by Jeff's good friend and hunting guide, Glenn Garner, who showed them the ropes as they made their way through the woods. It was very exciting for Gip and Richard to be hunting again. But they were especially thrilled to be with Jeff, as they enjoyed every minute of the fun and laughter he provided.

Gip did not get a deer that weekend, but he got a morale boost that could not be measured in words—or antlers. Gip and Glenn hit it off right

Jeff shows Gip his deer trophies.

Gip with Glenn Garner, just before they left for the woods to hunt.

away, and in yet another blessing from Jeff, Gip spent the following summer working with Glenn at Jeff's hunting farm. Glenn and his wife, Andrea, graciously invited Gip to stay with them while he worked on the farm.

Jeff's brother Jay joined them from time to time, and he and Gip became fast friends as well. It was an awesome summer for Gip being with these fine Christian men. They were incredible mentors to him, and he will forever treasure what he learned from each one.

People who think that miracles only happened in Biblical times don't know the story of Gip Gayle. . . . It has been a joy and honor to get to know Gip and his wonderful family. They have elevated my belief in the power of prayer.

—Jeff Foxworthy, comedian

CHAPTER 38

Catch Me if You Can

As Gip approached his second semester back at college, approximately a year and a half after his accident, we were beginning to feel the chaos in our lives settle down a bit. We weren't experiencing the urgency of being "on call" 24/7. And we were finally easing ourselves away from sleeping with one eye open.

Weeks later, Gip had a very unexpected seizure. He had not had one in almost a year, and we thought that concern was over. But this was a doozy, and it put us back on full alert. He was rushed to the nearest hospital by ambulance. Emergency-room physicians ran countless tests, scans, and lab workups. We waited for hours while they consulted with several of Gip's previous doctors. Once that was done, the ER docs made the decision to change Gip's medications and discharge him. We were relieved he was all right but concerned about the implications of it all.

The following week, Gip had another seizure. He was in the kitchen while I was down the hall carrying a laundry basket full of towels. I barely heard him say, "Mom, can you catch me?" He spoke just above a whisper, so I wasn't sure if I heard him right.

I dropped the basket and sped to the kitchen. As I rounded the corner, I saw Gip desperately trying to hold onto the kitchen island. He looked at me with a glazed-over stare as he began to shake. I rushed to his side, grabbed him with one arm and the kitchen island with the other, hoping it would hold us up. But we both began to fall, so I threw my body under his to provide some cushion that would protect his head. His whole body fell on top of mine, and we landed with a loud thump.

Fortunately, it was my head, not his, that hit the hardwood floor. As soon as he was able, we slowly crawled to the nearby sofa. I was too frightened to lift him or let him stand again until I knew he was all right. When we got to a safe and comfortable position, I gently lifted him onto the sofa.

We knew what that little episode meant and were heartsick over it. It was yet another reminder that setbacks were still a part of Gip's recovery. And with each setback came new concerns for his future.

As he rested on the sofa, I sat on the floor beside my precious child, and we both quietly wept. I wept like I do: with tears. Gip wept like he does: with a stoic stare of determination that this would *not* defeat him.

During the next few weeks, we met with several medical specialists. Under the direction of Dr. Leslie, they ran a gamut of blood tests, CT scans, and EEGs (brain wave tests) to be certain other problems were not developing. Dr. Leslie made certain that each doctor responded to this concern with great diligence, performing a broad spectrum of exams. He wanted no stone left unturned, going with a better-safe-than-sorry approach.

Fortunately, all test results were in Gip's favor. So the outcome was little more than a change in Gip's medications. Oh, how we breathed a sigh of relief for that blessing.

CHAPTER 39

Random Acts of Kindness

A Servant's Heart

Despite the difficulties we faced, we noticed the many times throughout our journey when God stopped by and left His calling card. During the first few months, our meals-on-wheels angels made their drop-off before we got home from the hospital each night. Knowing we'd be too exhausted to prepare a meal, they had it set out on our kitchen island. All we had to do was pick up a fork.

In addition to that, our mail was carefully laid out for us each day. Newspapers were neatly stacked in the corner of the room along with flowers, plants, and gifts that had been delivered to our home. Our yard was mowed and edged. Our dog was walked and fed.

Many who came by picked up laundry and returned it washed, folded, and pressed. Our home was cleaned, vacuumed, and dusted on a regular basis. Taylor's football, baseball, and wrestling uniforms were cleaned and ready for the next day's workout. Knowing the colossal mileage our cars were enduring with long hauls to and from the hospital, friends took our vehicles in for oil changes and tire rotations, allowing us to stay by Gip's side at all times.

Who does this? Honestly, we still don't know who was behind a lot of the kindness shown to our family. So our answer is, "God! God does this." He puts it in our hearts to help others, but it's up to us to answer that call. How blessed we were that so many did.

After Gip's accident, it was clear I would not be able to return to work anytime soon. Gip needed me day and night, and I couldn't and wouldn't be anywhere else. Life as we knew it was on hold.

Robotically we went through the motions each day, but we weren't really present. Someone could've changed out all the furniture in our house at that time, and I don't think we would've noticed. That's just how it was. We were in survival mode only. Past that, little else mattered.

But, like it or not, there were other concerns. As time went on, challenges began to mount higher and higher. Laundry was piling up, and so were the bills. Soon it became impossible to put it all on the back burner. We were facing serious medical debt and were going to have to deal with it eventually.

At one point, our cell phone service was cut off. You'd think we would've been more aware of our situation. You'd think we would've noticed bills with "Final Notice" plastered all over the statement. But we were in a fog for so long, many things got by us.

During our lengthy hospital stay, I carried a large bag to and from the hospital. My intent was to sift through the mail, bills, and get-well cards in that bag during Gip's therapy sessions or afternoon naps. But with our new lives came new responsibilities. Suddenly we were inundated with TBI reading materials. Any spare moment we had was spent reviewing information about our child's new medical needs so that we could become proper caretakers once our patient came home.

Aware of our exhaustion and financial woes, friends began to sort through our mail and pay a few of our utility bills. Can you imagine such a thing? In our chaotic state of mind, we didn't even notice that bills were missing. I'm not sure if what they did was legal or not, but we've decided not to press charges!

Chuck and others held fund-raisers to help with our devastating medical bills. Our friends, the Burdette and Gaines families, reached out to help with some of our other overwhelming expenses. Carrie Rebisa, our friend and office manager for our dentist, Dr. Karl Lugus, called with the practice's blessing, offering dental care at no cost. Still others extended a helping hand in whatever ways they were able. The abundance of kindness never ceased to amaze us.

We've tried to thank all who've helped our family, but many who reached out to us have chosen to remain anonymous all these years. Let me say this to you: We may not know your names, but our Heavenly Father does. So we shall continue to lift you in prayer "by deed," understanding that God knows you "by name." And no doubt He accepts our prayers for you and will bless you for your beautiful servant hearts.

Strides for Strength

Shortly after Gip came home from Shepherd Center, we received a call from a young man, a student from Gip's high school. He wanted to put on a five-kilometer (5K) benefit race for our son.

We were quite taken aback by this offer, especially from such a young person. We asked how he heard about Gip's accident, and he replied, "The whole world knows about Gip's accident, and we've all been praying for him." I was deeply moved by his words and began to choke up as we continued our conversation.

This young man, Rob Montepare, was only a junior in high school at the time, yet he'd already started a nonprofit organization, Strides for Strength. I remembered his first benefit, which was held for his friend Keaston White, who had been paralyzed in a football injury just two years earlier. We'd been praying for Keaston and his family, never imagining that *our* family would one day be dealing with a life-altering injury.

I thanked Rob for his kind offer, and several months later the race was on. Hundreds of people showed up to support Gip, including about forty of his fraternity brothers. Gip wasn't able to run the race, but he slowly walked a shortcut route and received a huge round of applause when he crossed the finish line.

Gip with Rob Montepare (center) and Keaston White.

Richard, Gip, Beth, and Taylor getting their 5K runner numbers before the race.

Family, friends, and fraternity brothers line up for the benefit race; overall, more than 200 supporters showed up!

Gip walks alongside as runners run the race.

Lend a Hand When You Can

About a month after the 5K race, I received a call from a few of my girlfriends. We are all very close at heart, sisters in many ways, and they had been faithfully by my side through each and every struggle. With hearts for God and a gift for helping others, they began planning a fund-raiser for our family.

They told me they had met with a local restaurant owner, Bill Green, to discuss hosting a dinner for our family. Gip's story touched the owner's heart so deeply that he said "count me in" even though he had never met Gip or our family. He agreed to help with the food as well as hosting the event at his restaurant.

Once Gip was able, we went to the restaurant to meet Bill and thank him for his kindness. Right away Bill and Gip began to fire away at each other with their witty quips. We knew then we'd be friends for life . . . and we are.

As my girlfriends gathered at the restaurant for meeting after meeting, they worked tirelessly planning every detail of this wonderful event. Each time they met, Bill referred to them as "Gip's Girls." The title caught on, and soon Jamie, Robin, Karyn, Wendy, and Angie became fondly known as "Gip's Girls." To this day my family refers to them by their stage name!

They titled their fund-raiser "Lend a Hand When You Can."

Family portrait taken for the "Lend a Hand When You Can" benefit.

Circle of friends lessens burden

'Gip's Girls' give financial, spiritual help to injured man and his family

VASNA WILSON / Staff

Gip Gayle and his family laugh at how, upon awakening from a three-day coma, Gip asked first about his dog, Yeller. A sense of humor has helped the family — and Gip — cope.

Newspaper article about the "Gip's Girls" benefit.

Gip gets a kiss from one of his Girls!

ABOVE: Gip with Bill Green.
RIGHT: Gip thanks everyone for
an amazing benefit.

Gip with Bill and Gip's Girls at a golf tournament benefit.

Uncle Tate's Crawfish Boil

Gip's twentieth birthday was on the horizon, and we were determined to make it special. But we were still limited by what he would be able to do. We asked Gip what he'd like for his birthday, and he immediately responded, "I want a Louisiana crawfish boil like we always have at Uncle Tate's house—the one I missed this year."

News traveled fast, and preparations began. The day before Gip's birthday, my brother Tate and sister-in-law Pam flew to Atlanta. They had nearly two hundred pounds of live crawfish flown in as well, enough to feed a crowd of family and friends. After hours of hard work cleaning, boiling, and seasoning to perfection, Tate and Pam shouted out, "Happy Birthday, Gipper. Let's eat crawfish!" Beaming the whole time, Gip ate one crawfish after another. But as happy as he was, I do believe that Tate and Pam were even happier. They stood with smiles on their faces and tears in their eyes as they soaked up Gip's joy. Ah . . . the gift of giving.

Taylor with Aunt Pam and Uncle Tate boiling the crawfish.

My parents (Honey and Pops) and one of my sisters, Helen (the singer), also came to town for this get-together. This was one of many trips for which Helen's loving husband, Dennis, stayed home in Texas to help with their children so she could fly to us whenever we needed her.

Having family with us, along with many friends and neighbors, made this quite a celebration. Helen entertained us by performing the song she wrote for Gip, "Miracle." And yes, we all cried. After all, we were there to celebrate not only Gip's birthday, but God's miracle in his life.

Aunt Helen singing her song, "Miracle."

Gip and Taylor with Chuck and his wife, Julie, wearing LSU doo rags in honor of Gip's birthday!

Gip and Taylor thanking Aunt Pam and Uncle Tate with the gift
of Richard's painting.

Have Truck, Will Travel

After making countless trips to work each day, to Shepherd Center each evening, and back home after that, Richard's truck finally gave out. He called me from the road, broken down in five o'clock traffic on a Friday afternoon on I-75, one of Atlanta's busiest highways. His truck had to be hauled to a repair shop where, unfortunately, it was declared unrepairable. Suddenly we needed to find another vehicle, and soon.

Shortly after I received Richard's call, Chuck called me to check on Gip. He heard the worry in my voice and asked what was wrong. I told him about Richard's truck and asked if he knew anyone wanting to sell a used vehicle. Chuck said he had a friend, Casey Coffey, owner of a local car dealership, Gwinnett Place Ford, who might have a used truck we could buy.

Thirty minutes later, I received a call from Casey. We talked about Richard's truck needs, and Casey said he would let us know if he found something of interest. I thanked him for his kindness, and we hung up.

Later that evening, Casey called back saying he might have a truck we would be interested in. The following morning, Richard, Gip, and I drove to the dealership. We asked about the price, but Casey said it was a trade-in, and he didn't have a cost yet.

He walked over to the truck and said, "Here it is. Do you like it?" It was a nice truck, so we felt it was probably out of our price range. Not knowing the cost made it awkward. So we thanked Casey and said we'd keep it in mind as we continued our search.

"Don't you like it?" Casey asked.

Trying to be gracious, Richard replied, "Sure, it looks like a great truck. I just don't think it fits what we need right now."

Casey continued to press. "But you like it, right?"

Richard acknowledged that it was a nice truck and asked again about the price.

Casey smiled and said, "It's *free!*"

We stood there for a moment, confused. Then Richard said, "I don't understand."

Casey explained that he and his family were some of Gip's prayer warriors. He said when he got the call from Chuck about our need for a vehicle, he knew God was giving him a chance to help.

Richard thanked Casey but explained that we could not accept such a gift. We offered to purchase the truck instead. This haggling went on for quite a while. But in the end, Casey refused, insisting that we were "stealing his joy" if we did not accept his gift.

Once again, our family was lifted by one of God's angels with a servant's heart. Amazing—simply amazing!

Richard, Gip, and Beth with Casey Coffey, offering the blessing of a great truck to get Richard back on the road.

Gip and Richard driving off the lot with grateful hearts.

No Kind Deed Goes Unnoticed

Early on during Gip's recovery time at Shepherd Center, I was walking toward his room after meeting with the neurosurgeon. Gip was having more complications, and I had just been told he would need yet another surgery. I was distraught.

As I neared Gip's hallway, I heard someone calling for me. "Beth, Beth, come here for a minute." Then, to someone else, "She's the mother." It was a group of Shepherd Center administrators walking with a gentleman whom I knew I recognized, but in my troubled frame of mind I couldn't recall who he was. They introduced me to the University of Georgia football coaching legend Vince Dooley. We shook hands, I said it was nice to meet him, and I turned around to leave.

They quickly called me back, saying that Coach Dooley would like to meet Gip. Apparently, Coach was there to visit a friend, and the hospital staff told him about one of their other patients: a young man, a huge college football fan, who'd suffered a traumatic brain injury from a hunting accident. They asked Coach if he could take a few minutes to say hello and lift this young man's spirits. He graciously accepted their request, and they were headed to Gip's room when they saw me in the hall.

Not knowing of this visit in advance, I had no time to prepare Gip. So as we walked into the room together, I said, "Gip, you have a very special visitor. This is . . ."

But before I could finish my sentence, Gip's eyes lit up, and he said, "Hey, Coach Dooley!"

Wow! Even in his weakened, fragile state, Gip knew a Hall of Fame football coach when he saw one. Everyone was impressed by Gip's cognizance.

With that, Coach reached out to shake Gip's hand. Gip was not able to move very well at that time but somehow managed to lift his arm enough to shake back. Having been told that Gip was a former Georgia high school football player and a big college football fan, Coach Dooley immediately said, "Gip, I bet you're a Georgia Bulldog fan, right?"

Without skipping a beat Gip replied, "Um, no sir, Coach. I'm an LSU fan! Look around my room."

Coach Dooley turned his head and quickly realized that Gip's hospital room was covered with LSU decor—banners, flags, photos, footballs, and baseballs. Now, you have to remember that this was in the fall of 2003, and LSU had beaten Georgia that season. This could've been ugly!

I can't imagine that Gip's team spirit made Coach Dooley very fond of our LSU-loving family. But nonetheless, he very graciously leaned over the bed and told Gip that it was okay. He said that his son, Derek, was actually one of the coaches on the LSU football staff that year. He told Gip that he couldn't help but be proud and happy for his son. We had a good laugh about the irony of it all, and then I took a photo of Gip and Coach Dooley as a remembrance of his kindness.

Given his condition at the time, Gip wasn't able to show much excitement. But meeting the legendary Coach Vince Dooley meant a lot to him and brought great joy to us on a day when we really needed it. Instead of concentrating on the gut-wrenching news of another surgery, we quickly changed our focus to the day's highlight—meeting a Hall of Famer.

As soon as Coach left the room, Gip wanted to call his dad to tell him about meeting Vince Dooley. We also called a few of Gip's football friends to share the great news. Gip was too weak to talk to everyone, so I made the calls for him. As I shared his exciting day with family and friends, Gip lay in bed grinning from ear to ear.

At that time, we thought it would be the last of our connection with Coach Dooley. But nearly two years later, he was nearby at a signing session for his new book, *Dooley: My 40 Years at Georgia*. When we heard about it, Gip said, "Mom, I'd like to shake his hand and thank him again for coming to see me at Shepherd Center. He has no idea how much that meant to me." I agreed.

Before we left, we grabbed a copy of the photo we'd taken at the hospital to remind Coach Dooley how they had met. Our goal was simply to say "thank you again" and let him know that his act of kindness went a long way.

At the signing, we bought a book and stood in line with other football fans anxious to have him sign their books. When it was our turn, Coach said hello and reached for Gip's book, asking how he wanted the book to be signed.

There was a slight pause, as Gip was a bit choked up. But then he said, "Coach, I'm mainly here to thank you for visiting me at Shepherd Center a couple of years ago. And if you don't mind, I'd like to have you write 'Go Tigers' in my book!"

Coach Dooley lifted his head with a puzzled expression. So I quickly stepped in and showed Coach the photo of him with Gip at Shepherd Center and told him that we will always treasure how he lifted Gip's spirits that day.

He looked at the photo, looked at me, and then looked back at Gip and said, "I remember you, young man." He paused for a moment as he glanced back at the photo and said, "You weren't doing too well back then. They weren't sure you were going to make it. Look at you now!"

I got all teary-eyed and asked if we could possibly get another photo of him with Gip. To which he quickly replied, "I'd be honored."

Coach's book-signing manager was not too thrilled, because the line was quite long and time was running out. He motioned to Coach that there really wasn't time for photos, and they needed to move on to other customers. Coach Dooley looked at him and said very clearly, "I have time for *this* young man!" He then got out of his chair and walked to the end of the table, where I quickly snapped another photo. He shook Gip's hand again and thanked him for coming by.

To this day, proudly displayed in Gip's bedroom are the hospital photo and the book-signing photo, along with Coach Dooley's book—signed "Go Tigers!"

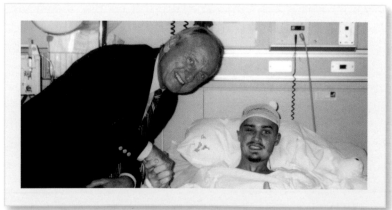

Coach Dooley pays a hospital visit to Gip.

Coach Dooley's inscription in Gip's book.

Purpose of Giving

It is my hope that sharing stories of the compassion shown to our family—the random acts of kindness—may spark something within all of us, me included, about how we can help others.

Our lives were carefully put back together by those who said "yes" to God's prompting. They could've easily said "no," and no one would've ever known. But where would we be?

So often we think we have nothing to give, but that's simply not true. Even if we don't have time, talent, or treasure to offer, we can still bring hope, help, and humor. And let's not forget the power of "food ministry"! We know, only too well, that even the smallest acts of kindness can reach the deepest needs. One gift is not of greater value than the other. For it was as a whole that our family was restored.

If you feel a pressing on your heart to help someone, remember this: That still, small voice in our heads and hearts is our Heavenly Father tugging on our heartstrings for a reason. He needs to use our hands and feet to do His work. We should listen when He speaks, act when He calls upon us, and be blessed when He shows us the way.

When I think about how many helping hands reached out to us, I am reminded of one of my most treasured childhood memories. While just a little girl, I was at church one Sunday morning when the offering basket was being passed down our pew. My dad put in his monetary gift as he always had.

I had never really thought about it before, but this time I was curious and wondered how much money he had given. I whispered in his ear, "Daddy, how do you know how much to give when the basket comes around?"

I was too young to understand the concept of tithing, so my dad smiled and hugged me as he said, "That's easy, sweetheart. You give more than you can spare. That's when it's really giving." Thanks for that beautiful lesson, Daddy.

Our family has certainly witnessed what *really* giving is all about. We've seen people go out of their way to help, giving more than they could spare. Together they helped make us whole again.

CHAPTER 40

"One for the Gipper"

As we neared the two-year anniversary of Gip's accident, he received a call from Jeff Foxworthy. Jeff called to say he felt led by God to do a benefit concert in Gip's honor.

Once again, Jeff's kindness overwhelmed Gip. He graciously thanked Jeff but said that he couldn't accept such a gift. Jeff responded in typical Foxworthy fashion, saying, "Gipper, I'm just telling you when it's gonna happen, buddy, and it would be great if you could be there!" Yep, humor is the best medicine, and Jeff is the best at it. He called the event "One for the Gipper."

Before Jeff called Gip, he had contacted Chuck to talk about his idea to be sure it would not embarrass Gip or our family in any way, because that is just the kind of considerate man Jeff is. The timing of Jeff's call to Chuck was almost eerie in that the night before, Chuck woke in the morning's wee hours with thoughts of talking to Jeff about possibly doing a benefit for Gip. Chuck scribbled a note on the pad on his nightstand to remind himself to speak with Jeff the next day.

The following morning, Chuck told his wife of his restless night and what had kept him awake. He went about his day, but that night Jeff called, saying that he'd like to bounce a big idea off of him. Chuck hadn't spoken to Jeff in several months but said he had a strange feeling he knew what the idea was. Jeff told Chuck he was "weirding him out a little" and then shared his idea of doing a benefit for Gip. Jeff and Chuck quickly related the common vision to their wives, and they all marveled at the clarity of God's direction.

It took months of hard work to put this benefit together. Jeff's amazing managers and the wonderful Gwinnett Arena staff donated their time and services. Jeff's brother Jay was an angel as well. He worked endless hours managing the event, giving his time and talent to make certain it was a big success.

When the show began, our family was seated close to the stage. Chuck sat next to Gip. Extended family members and friends surrounded us on every side, taking up several large sections of the arena. As a special surprise

LOCAL EVENT • GWINNETT DAILY POST • FRIDAY, JULY 15, 2005

one for the Gipper

Comedian Jeff Foxworthy will perform at 8 p.m. today at the Arena at Gwinnett Center.

A newspaper spotlights Jeff Foxworthy's "One for the Gipper" benefit concert.

to Gip, his life-flight nurse and flight paramedic drove all the way from Savannah to join us for the concert. It was quite a reunion when they arrived.

Nearly eight thousand people attended this glorious event. Jeff was hilarious as always during his comedy routine. He was also kind enough to add several references to Gip throughout his act, personalizing the show for our family. At the performance's end, Jeff stood at the microphone and paused for a moment as he changed his persona from humor to heart.

He told the audience why his benefit was called "One for the Gipper." He briefly explained about Gip's accident and God's amazing grace in his recovery. He then told the story of how the two of them met . . . over a hat.

As Jeff finished speaking, a huge drop-down screen appeared behind him, and he explained that he wanted to share a brief video of Gip's journey, accompanied by the song "Miracle," written by Gip's aunt. My heart was overcome seeing the photos of our son's journey and hearing my sister's angelic voice ringing through the rafters.

After the video, Jeff walked back onstage and said, "I've never seen him without a smile, ladies and gentlemen. Please help me welcome my friend, Gip Gayle, a walking miracle!" Gip slowly walked on stage to a standing ovation. It was clear he was quite taken aback by the standing O, and without realizing it, he literally took a step back!

Jeff waved him back onto the stage. Gip walked over to Jeff, and they hugged as Jeff motioned for Gip to look at the audience clapping for him. Gip told Jeff, "Man, there sure are a lot of people here." Jeff busted out laughing and told the audience what Gip said. Everyone continued to clap, so Gip nervously stood there and gave a little wave of thanks for the overwhelming reception.

He was barely able to breathe, let alone speak. But he dug deep and found the courage to address the crowd, thanking Jeff, Chuck, and his prayer warriors.

Gip thanks Jeff for his kindness and generosity.

Gip on stage thanking Chuck, family, and friends for their prayers and support.

As I recall this part of our journey, I can't help but tear up. My body shivers as I think about this blessed moment in our lives. I remember Richard's stoic smile as he fought to hold back the tears. He put his arm around me, and our bodies shook together as we soaked in the pure joy of it all.

Filled with emotion, I blurted out my heart's thoughts as I shouted, "Thank you, Jesus!" Many heads turned when they heard me scream such praise. But it was both scream-worthy and praiseworthy. This was the greatest night of our lives, and we knew where that gift came from.

Gip with Jeff and Chuck after the show.

The Gayles with Jeff, Gregg, Jordan, and Jules Foxworthy.

Gip with Alison Herrington and Jeff Clifton, who
drove in from Savannah for the benefit.

Long before we met Jeff, he was a part of helping Gip, indirectly. At Shepherd Center, Gip's therapists (also Foxworthy fans) used Jeff's trademark redneck jokes as an incentive to get Gip through his daily challenges. With Foxworthy humor, they kept him amused to cajole him to sit up a little longer, eat another bite of lunch, read another sentence, and take another step. They had a daily competition to see who could remember the most redneck jokes. Gip, with his competitive spirit and love for Foxworthy humor, usually won, or so he says!

Many days that humor was the only thing that could lift Gip's spirits. On his last day at Shepherd Center, his therapists gave him a going-home gift: the

The moment I laid eyes on Gip, every ounce of my being prayed that we would be able to get him to Savannah alive and to the trauma team that was waiting for him. Since then many miracles have unfolded before my eyes as I have witnessed the steadfast faith of Gip and the Gayle family. We've kept in touch and have remained close friends. Because of Gip and his family, my life and faith have been forever changed.

—Alison Herrington, flight nurse for LifeStar One
helicopter ambulance service in Savannah, Georgia

Gip and Taylor with Jay Foxworthy.

Gip and Jeff enjoying a glorious night.

2004 Foxworthy Redneck joke calendar. Unbeknownst to anyone at the time, Gip would have his very own redneck joke in the following year's calendar.

Got chills yet? There's more.

As further encouragement, Gip's therapists promised to take him to a Jeff Foxworthy performance once he was able to travel. Gip told them he would hold them to that promise. Well, almost two years later they *were* at a Foxworthy show together, but never in their wildest dreams had any of them thought it would be a "One for the Gipper" show.

Having been fans of Jeff Foxworthy, our family was starstruck when we met him. Now that we've gotten to know Jeff on a personal level, our admiration has been trumped by inspiration as we've watched the way he and his family live such Christian lives.

We've been blessed to get to know Jeff's beautiful wife, Gregg, and their precious daughters, Jordan and Jules. Gregg invited me to join her Bible study group, and that has given us a chance to bond even more. I've come to see that her beauty is both inside and out. It is *that* trait of the Foxworthy family that we're the most proud to know and love.

Jeff has been a dear friend to our family. He has touched our hearts, tickled our funny bones, and inspired our souls. We have thanked him and Gregg many times, but they will never really know just how much their kind and generous hearts have blessed our lives.

CHAPTER 41

Hunt of a Lifetime

D uring Gip's recovery at home, we had a lot of downtime, resting for long periods each day. We spent hours watching television to pass the time. Being a sports fanatic, Gip watched many sporting events, games, and hunting shows.

One day we happened upon a program showing a Hunt of a Lifetime hunt. We watched a teenage boy enjoying what ended up being his final hunt.

As the narrator told of the boy's bout with cancer, I could see Gip wincing. He clearly related to this young man. Their medical crises differed, but there were a lot of similarities in the dramatic changes to their lives. Gip understood the pain, heartache, and fear this teenager dealt with.

My first instinct was to change the channel, but Gip wouldn't let me. We watched the hunt and saw this young man's heartwarming smile when he showed off his prize-winning buck. The narrator's voice cracked when he shared the sad news that the teenager had passed away a few months later. Gip turned his head toward me, choked up a bit, and asked, "Mom, do you think I'll ever be able to go on a dream hunt like that?"

After all we'd been through, I wasn't exactly fond of hunting. But hearing Gip's hope to one day hunt like that stirred my heart deeply. Knowing these were private hunts gave me comfort for his safety. So I secretly contacted the Hunt of a Lifetime organization online, filled in its application, and waited to see where it might lead.

Hunt of a Lifetime was founded by Tina Pattison, a mom who started the organization in her son's memory. At age nineteen, Tina's son Matt had been diagnosed with Hodgkin's disease. His lifelong dream was to hunt moose in Canada. As hunters in the area learned about Matt's wish, they gathered together to make it come true. With little time, but much determination and the kindness of many, Matt went to Canada and came home with his moose trophy. Shortly after his hunt, Matt lost his battle with cancer. Soon after, his mom created the Hunt of a Lifetime (HOAL) Foundation.

Weeks after I filled out the HOAL request form, I received a call from Tina. She wanted to know all about Gip, his accident, and his injuries. She asked what Gip's hunting dreams were, what animals he'd like to hunt, and where. I had not done my homework. Not knowing if we'd ever be contacted by HOAL, I never mentioned it to Gip. I didn't want to build his hopes in case they never called.

Well, they called. And suddenly this was becoming a reality. Richard and Gip agreed it would be quite an expedition to go out West and hunt for elk and mule deer. Within weeks, HOAL flew them both to Sun Valley, Idaho.

By this time it had been a little over two years since Gip's accident. He had never even dreamed of something like this, yet here it was. Things were happening so fast, it didn't seem real. Gip was overwhelmed with joy. But in hunting there are no guarantees, so he and Richard had to keep their expectations in check because they might come home empty-handed.

Upon arrival, they met with the Idaho state ambassadors for HOAL, Lorna and Brian Hamel. They treated Gip and Richard like family. We remain close friends to this day.

The next morning, the hunt began. Gip and Richard met with Robert, the hunting guide. They saddled their horses and headed to the Pioneer Mountains of the Sawtooth National Forest for several days of a pack 'n' hunt adventure.

Gip and Richard before the Hunt of a Lifetime.

Checking the mules before the hunt.

As they rode into the thick of the mountains, they spotted a six-by-six bull elk, with six points on each massive antler. Gip took about five shots but missed. His body slumped with disappointment, but Robert told him there would be more chances. It began to get dark, so they had to stop the hunt to set up camp. They put up their tents, ate by the campfire, and rested for the next day's journey.

The following morning, they loaded the pack mules, mounted their horses, and set out on a three-hour ride to the next hunting area. Once there, they began their cow call to see if a bull was nearby. Much to their surprise, one bugled back, and the romance began. They saw his massive body top a ridge about three hundred yards away, so they nestled into position in some nearby sagebrush.

Because of his injury, Gip's doctors insisted he wear special ear protection during the hunt. So he put on the ear gear and got ready to shoot. Robert whispered to Gip to wait until he drew the bull in a little closer for a better shot, but with the ear protection, Gip didn't hear him. He fired the moment he spotted the elk. From over three hundred yards away, Gip dropped the elk with one shot. "You got him, Gipper, you got him!" Robert shouted. I don't know who was more excited: Gip, Richard, or Robert.

At first Gip was speechless. He kept hugging his dad and asking if it was real. The elk was indeed a fine animal: a seven-by-seven bull elk, weighing approximately eight hundred pounds. After their high-fives and

Saddled up and ready to go.

Gip and Richard with Gip's royal elk.

back-slapping, they took off their hats, bowed their heads, and said the Hunter's Prayer, thanking God for the blessing of the harvest.

The following day they headed back out to continue Gip's dream hunt. This time they were hunting for a mule deer. They spent twelve hours riding horseback over rugged terrain. They saw about ten does but never spotted anything with horns. Dusk approached, and they had to call it a night. The hunting guide told them mule deer were much harder to hunt than elk. Anxiety began to set in, and so did exhaustion, especially for Gip.

They rose early the next morning, ate breakfast, and packed up camp. Tired and realizing it might be another long day in the saddle, the group was not as hopeful as it had been the day before. They had only one more day to hunt. Determined to keep the hope alive, they said a prayer before they left.

About an hour into the ride, the guide signaled that he spotted something. Richard held the horses and mules back while Gip moved closer. When he looked through the scope and realized how massive the buck's rack was, he almost passed out. Gip quickly focused on the target, put his finger on the trigger, and took a shot. At first he didn't know if he got him or

Gip and Richard with Gip's mule deer.

not, but when the congratulatory screaming began Gip knew another dream had come true. He had shot a seventeen-point mule deer.

After the hunt, Lorna and Brian set up a church youth group meeting for the local teens to meet Gip and hear his testimony. He was nervous but shared his story with these kids the best way he knew how—from his heart.

On the last night in Idaho, HOAL held a "Feast of the Beast" celebration with a special menu that included some of Gip's elk and mule deer meat. It was a great opportunity for Gip and Richard to express their gratitude to the many locals who helped make this dream hunt a reality. Gip shared his appreciation, saying he would never forget this amazing hunt or their kindness that made it all possible. Richard wrapped up the night by describing their experience like this: "In animal terms, Gip came to Idaho as a black bear, but thanks to all of you, he's leaving as a grizzly! God bless you."

HOAL shipped the rest of Gip's elk and deer meat to our home, and we continued to feast on his harvest. Several months later, he received his trophies—professionally mounted elk and deer heads. He was so excited he could hardly wait to hang them. Everyone who enters our home admires these treasures, but for Gip they are a reminder of a dream come true!

Gip giving his testimony to a local youth group in Idaho.

At home with the mule deer trophy mount.

With the royal elk trophy mount.

CHAPTER 42

Journey of Forgiveness

From day one, we opened our hearts to the young man who had accidentally shot our son. We extended the same warmth to his family. We prayed with them, and we cried with them. We even laughed together at times as we shared our humorous sides. It was the only way we knew to handle such a fragile situation. This was a tragedy, and both families were hurting in immeasurable ways.

As Gip began to show signs of improvement, we talked about spending the upcoming Thanksgiving together so we could celebrate the miracles God was performing. We swapped phone numbers and kept in touch regularly during the first couple of months. At his parents' request, we encouraged their son to get counseling to help him through this difficult time. We often talked about how awesome it was that we were lifting each other up.

The way we reached out to this young man and his family was genuine. We had no energy to put on an act. As family and friends were praying for our family, we asked them to pray for his family as well. We *all* needed prayers.

After we left Savannah and moved back to Atlanta, we encouraged the young man and his family to come see Gip as often as they could. They visited Shepherd Center a couple of times, and the young man came to our home a few times after that. But months later, he faded out of our lives.

It's not that we didn't "get it," because we did. We knew it had to be difficult for him to watch Gip go through so much suffering. We knew he was dealing with a whole different kind of suffering. But we also knew that Gip had forgiven him and asked him to be a part of his recovery.

On his first visit after the accident, the young man asked Gip if he could forgive him. Gip assured him of his forgiveness and said, "Let's get through this together, and we'll both be stronger men for it." Our family felt that getting through it together would be the best way for both families to heal. But that was not to be.

When I began writing about our journey, I did not want to include *how* this tragedy happened. Our family had buried that heartache years ago, and

I did not want to dig it up. But I've continued to feel a deep pressing to share our journey of forgiveness in all this. That forgiveness involves reviewing the details of what led up to that fateful moment in our son's life.

That's quite an emotional task. But I've decided that if sharing the lessons we've learned can possibly help others through *their* journey of forgiveness—and perhaps even save lives as it sheds light on the importance of hunter safety—then it is the right and responsible thing to do. Here's what happened.

When the Department of Natural Resources (DNR) law-enforcement officers arrived on the scene, they began questioning the hunters at the site. According to the Georgia Hunting Incident Report, the shooter was the only eyewitness. DNR officers questioned the young man who shot our son and discovered that he had never taken the state-mandated Hunter's Safety Course. Without a Safety Course certificate number, the shooter would have been denied a hunting license. If proof of a valid hunting license had been required before the hunt began, the shooter would not have been allowed to hunt that day.

Several days later, DNR officers arrived at the Savannah hospital with their preliminary police report of the hunting incident. Even though this was clearly an accident, they kept referring to it as an *incident*. The officers informed us that the shooter had not taken a Hunter's Safety Course and that their office would be running an investigation of the incident.

In the official Georgia Hunting Incident Report, the shooter states that he was sitting on a camouflaged stool, approximately twenty-six feet to Gip's right. He reports that as they were watching for doves, he had his firearm across his lap, with the barrel pointed in Gip's direction. He goes on to say that a bird was approaching from the southeastern part of the dove field, and as he was raising his gun, it went off.

According to the report, when the bird was in range, the shooter began raising his shotgun, with the muzzle pointed in Gip's direction and his finger on the trigger, causing the gun to fire before it was shouldered, striking our son on the right side of his head.

The DNR officer acknowledged that while securing the shotguns, he noticed that the safety of the shooter's gun was in the "fire" position; that is, the gun's safety was off. Firearm scientists were contacted to test the gun. Their report concluded that the shotgun was in good working condition, functioning as designed.

The incident report also notes that the victim was covered by the shooter "swinging on the game." In laymen's terms, this means that as the shooter was tracking the dove's flight from left to right, he had not cleared Gip from his gun sights and was therefore still aiming in Gip's direction as he followed the dove.

Hunter safety experts have shared with us that if the shooter had been properly trained, this tragedy could have been prevented. They say if he had followed even *one* of the safety precautions taught in the Hunter Safety Course, our son would not have been shot that day.

Had the shooter's gun not been pointed in Gip's direction while they were seated, chances are the gun would not have been raised up facing Gip. Had the gun safety been in the "on" position, he could not have accidentally fired the shotgun, even with his finger on the trigger. Had the shooter harnessed the shotgun on his shoulder before he put his finger on the trigger, the shot would've gone over Gip's head. And had the shooter cleared Gip from his gun sights before he began swing shooting, he would not have hit our son. This is why the law requires hunters to take the safety course *before* they are allowed to hunt.

As the officers presented diagrams and layouts of the hunting field, showing the proximity of where the hunters were seated, they shared their initial conclusions with us. We were in no shape to read at that time, so someone read the report out loud to us. We acknowledged their findings and thought that was the end of it.

But more than a year and a half later, we received a call from an investigative officer in the district attorney's office informing us that they were finalizing their investigation of the September 2003 shooting incident involving our son. Having had no contact with law enforcement officials since their visit to the Savannah hospital just days after the accident, we were stunned to get such a call. We immediately responded, saying, "We don't understand. We're not pressing charges against this young man."

The investigator was very kind and professional as he informed us that it was their job to protect and serve the public. He clarified that he was calling not to ask our permission to pursue the investigation, but rather to notify us, as the victim's family, that their office planned to continue the inquiry into the hunting incident that severely injured our son.

We questioned why this was being pursued nearly two years after the accident. We have since learned that the initial investigation had never been closed. Because of the ongoing severity of Gip's medical condition, investigators were unable to obtain an official statement from him. For a long time, serious concerns existed as to whether Gip would ultimately survive the shooting. His survival could bring up possible charges of firearm negligence, but a fatality could lead to more serious charges.

The DA's investigator requested medical records and physician statements from Gip's hospitals and doctors. They also requested an outline of Gip's current condition and prognosis. They continued to pursue their investigation and sent subpoenas ordering Gip and me to testify before the grand jury.

Gip had just left for his first trip away from home since his accident. He was with Chuck, serving as a volunteer at a YL Christian summer camp for kids. I had to drive four hours to pick him up from camp, and we then had to travel another six hours to the courthouse to appear before the grand jury.

After we arrived, the process took several hours. It was difficult for Gip to be on the witness stand answering detailed questions about what took place before he was shot. He choked up several times and paused to gather his composure. I wasn't allowed in the courtroom when he was being questioned, so I couldn't hear what he was saying. But I peeked through the blinds and was able to see how he was doing. It was painful to watch him struggle, but at least I knew he was all right.

Gip's doctors were concerned that the stress from this ordeal could cause him to have another seizure. He was clearly shaken by the experience but was able to walk unassisted out of the courtroom. When he entered the waiting area, we embraced in a long, emotional hug.

The judge called me in next. The questions they asked were mainly related to Gip's medical conditions and his long-term prognosis. I, too, became very emotional as I did my best to describe the challenges Gip had faced and will continue to face.

Finally it was over, and we were allowed to leave the courthouse. It was late, and we needed to rest, but Gip and I decided we'd rather face the long drive back than stay any longer. So off we went.

Several days later, we received a call from the DA's investigator informing us that the state had filed charges against the shooter. He was charged with one felony count of negligent misuse of a firearm while hunting resulting in severe bodily harm, and three misdemeanors related to not having taken the Hunter's Safety Education Course and hunting without a license.

By this time, nearly a year had passed since we had heard from this young man or his family. But after these charges were filed, they tried to contact us. We did not respond because our legal counsel advised us not to. We knew, however, that they must have been frightened by this unexpected turn of events. So we asked the court system if there was anything we could do to help this young man. They informed us that we could write a "Family of the Victim" letter to the judge asking for mercy on the defendant and requesting that he not serve any prison time. We did this right away.

The case never actually made it to trial, but it took the courts nearly six months to hash it all out. When the sentencing was over, the DA's representative called to tell us that the judge had taken our "Family of the Victim" letter into consideration and that the state's charges had been reduced because of it. They lowered the felony to a misdemeanor, and the shooter was charged with four misdemeanor counts. He did not serve a day in prison, nor will he have a felony record.

We understood the reason for this legal pursuit, as the authorities were trying to prevent a similar tragedy from happening to others. We certainly don't want anyone else to suffer as we have, so we honor and respect their position. Certainly, we too are strong advocates for hunter safety, encouraging it whenever and wherever we can.

But this was a lengthy ordeal, and a very emotional experience for our family. We were thankful when it was all over.

As we continued to shoulder the long-term trauma in Gip's recovery, family and friends watched us fight for our lives as we watched our child fight for his. As loved ones helped us care for Gip and Taylor, they also nursed us through *our* migraines, ulcers, and heart conditions. Numerous times, they've seen us fall out from exhaustion, tremble in fear, and cry ourselves to sleep.

Having witnessed our pain and suffering up close, many have asked how we could possibly forgive someone who caused such devastation in our lives.

Well, this was clearly an accident. We all know that. This young man did not intentionally hurt our son, his friend. He is a good kid who comes from a loving family. We bonded with them many times early on through a shared faith and a deep love for our sons. This accident was difficult for both families, and we all understood that.

But there *were* harsh realities that led to this life-altering event, and it could have been prevented. We've had to live with that tormenting truth through some very difficult years.

We almost lost our son more times than I can bear to recall. The ripple effect from this tragedy is immeasurable; that one shot wounded our *entire* family—emotionally, physically, and financially.

In an effort to keep our sanity—and move forward, not backward—we've had to remain positive in every aspect of Gip's recovery. By God's grace, we've been able to make peace with the fact that our son was shot, and with *how* he was shot. But it's been a journey.

Each time Gip faces another crisis or has another mountain to climb in his recovery, we have to hold on tight to our faith and to our forgiveness. We've come to realize that forgiveness is simple, but complicated; complicated, but simple.

We recognize that if we are going to ask for forgiveness in *our* failures, we must forgive others in *theirs*. We also know that an unforgiving spirit usually hurts the heart of the withholder. So for us, forgiveness has not been an option; it's been a must.

We have forgiven this young man. We do not harbor ill feelings or anger toward him. There's simply no place for that in our lives. We prayed for this young man in the beginning and continue to pray for him to this day.

Several months after the sentencing, our paths crossed again when Gip's fraternity Big Brother, Eric Crenshaw, tragically passed away. Eric and his family had been a wonderful support to Gip throughout his recovery, and we had grown to love them dearly. Gip was asked to be a pallbearer, and we attended the funeral to support the Crenshaw family and Eric's precious fiancée, Cori.

Eric was greatly loved, so hundreds of young men and women drove in for his funeral. Many were fraternity brothers, including the young man who accidentally shot Gip.

It was awkward to see him again after all this time. It became even more uncomfortable as we felt the stares of onlookers wondering how the reaction would be. But Gip soon remedied that. Richard and I watched as he walked over to the young man and reached for a handshake. The two said their hellos and chatted for a few minutes.

As the young man walked away, he looked toward us. We smiled and gave a little wave as we started to walk over to him. But we soon lost him in the crowd.

CHAPTER 43

Making Good on
a Promise

As we passed the two-year anniversary in Gip's recovery, he was improving at a remarkable pace. That's when he felt it was time to make good on a promise he'd made years earlier: to give his testimony at Chuck's church.

Chuck walked up to the altar but could barely get Gip's name out of his mouth without choking up. I do believe Chuck was as proud of him as Richard and I were. He gave a little introduction, and we all wept as Gip walked up to the altar.

He stood at the podium for a few seconds and took a deep breath. Gip was not used to public speaking. His accident didn't turn him into a storyteller, but it did turn him into someone with a story to tell, and he understands that.

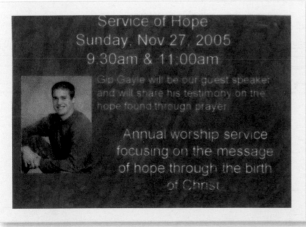

Chuck's church bulletin announcing Gip's testimony.

With hands shaking, palms sweating, and knees knocking, Gip courageously pushed through his stage fright. He started by thanking God, Chuck, and his prayer warriors for helping him get his life back. He then told a little about his accident and the challenges he faced. But he focused on how God got him through it and how God continues to guide him through the aftermath of such a life-altering event.

It was moving and emotional for everyone there, including Gip.

Gip and family with Chuck, Jeff and Jay Foxworthy,
and church pastors after Gip's testimony at Chuck's church.

Upon hearing about Gip's accident and his public-speaking prospects, a Dale Carnegie Training representative, Rod Eckard, whom we'd never met before, offered Gip a scholarship for the world-renowned speaking course.

Since then, Gip has had opportunities to speak to church ministries, Young Life events, Fellowship of Christian Athlete meetings, hunting clubs, and hospital gatherings. He's received many letters thanking him for sharing his story, saying that hearing how he overcame *his* tough times helped them overcome *theirs*.

Gip volunteered as a YL leader during Taylor's high school years, which gave him a chance to speak to that organization's groups as well. It was wonderful to see Gip and Taylor enjoying the gift of YL together. This leadership role gave Gip an opportunity to share his faith with Taylor and Taylor's friends in ways he never had before.

It's astounding the blessings that can come from the battles.

My friend Gip is an extraordinary person. His triumph through this tragedy is a testament to his strong character and a faith that was present long before the accident. His journey through this ordeal made others around him stronger and gave us all a reason to believe. I love Gip Gayle; he's like a son to me. He has taught me more about perseverance, hard work, and the power of prayer than anyone in my life. Gip is the real angel in this story. He is the true miracle—a faithful fighter who never gave up. He made us all believe!

—Chuck Scott, Gip's high school football coach
and Young Life Christian youth group mentor.

CHAPTER 44

Not Exactly a Speedy Recovery

Several months after Gip's testimony, a CT scan revealed that a portion of his skull-bone graft had begun to break down and was being absorbed into his body. That left a section of Gip's brain unprotected, and he faced another major surgery because of it.

After several medical consultations, the doctors decided to graft a section of bone from Gip's rib cage to cover the defect area. They explained that it would be a mean surgery, followed by a lengthy and painful recovery. And, as always, there were risks.

We tried to remain positive, but this was a crushing blow. Gip had been working so hard to move forward with his life. After he'd come so far, it was no small feat to overcome the disappointment of putting life on hold . . . again.

It had been about two years since Gip's last surgery and about two and a half years since his accident. We thought we were beyond this kind of setback. It was heartbreaking to think of Gip facing more hardships. We could not imagine going back to those stressful days when we found ourselves putting milk in the pantry and foil in the fridge.

I can remember thinking, "Surely this isn't happening." I felt that we had long since met our quota of hard times. But life doesn't work that way. We were back in the trenches fighting another battle in a war we thought we'd already won.

Chuck sent an email to Gip's prayer warriors. Like us, many had thought we were past this level of medical care, medical *scare*. But they lined up like the faithful angels they are and began their devoted prayers all over again.

The rib surgery turned out to be one of Gip's most painful. He remained in bed and in pain for several weeks. We were back to round-the-clock nursing care as we administered medications and changed bandages, all the while staying on high alert for symptoms of infection or rejection. I returned to my makeshift bed in the upstairs hallway.

Exhaustion crept back into our daily lives. We were dealing with a new crisis on the heels of one from which we'd just begun to recover, and we were running out of steam. We took many deep breaths as we prayed for God's strength to sustain us.

It took about a month for Gip to fully recuperate from this surgery, but he was able to return to college the following semester and pick up where he left off. We did our best to keep him healthy and hold our fears at bay.

For the next two years, he continued to recover at home. He attended classes at a local college, taking one or two courses each semester, and he worked hard on his study skills. He also spent a great deal of time at the gym.

Gip's energy level was nowhere near what it once was. The doctors said he needed to be working out every muscle group in order to rebuild his body strength and stamina. They wanted him to spend at least forty-five minutes on the treadmill each day. This was a tall order for someone who had been bedridden for so long. But Gip was determined to get back in shape, so he pushed himself further and further each day.

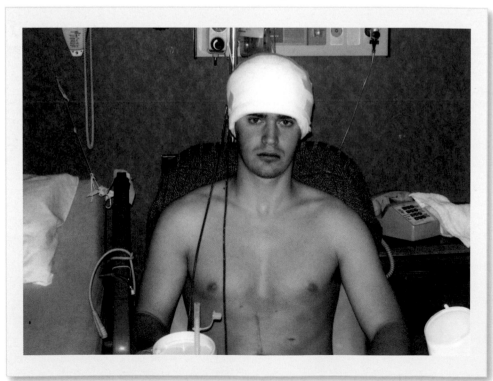

Gip after his rib-skull surgery.

Jason Vance, owner of a local gym, Body Plex, kindly offered Gip and our family lifetime memberships to ensure that Gip would come as often as possible without concern for cost. Being able to work out at a professional gym has been an important part of Gip's return to his old self. As many people know, working out is a lift not only to our bodies but to our spirits as well. Having this gym membership made it possible for Gip to restore both his muscle tone and his self-confidence.

It wasn't long before Gip was managing and organizing his own time and schedule. As he became more and more independent, we realized it was an *ongoing* miracle we were praying for. Gip wasn't looking just to survive; he wanted his life back. And he was going to do everything he possibly could to get it.

In the meantime, as parents, we were trying to keep Taylor's life on track as well. His world was filled with school activities, sporting events, homecoming dances and proms, getting his driver's license, going to YL summer camps, and so much more. We did our

Taylor's Collins Hill High School football photo.

Taylor with his new purchase—his first car!

Taylor dressed for the prom, with his second family—David Isbill and parents Jan and Edward Isbill.

Taylor and Gip playing volleyball at YL camp.

Taylor and Gip at camp where Gip served as volunteer YL leader.

best to provide as much normalcy as possible, but with the ongoing chaos and uncertainty we lived with, it was a struggle. Fortunately Taylor is a strong and resilient young man, and he somehow found a way to live faithfully and even joyfully through some very challenging times.

The road to recovery has been long, tough, and debilitating at times for all of us. For several years our hearts raced back and forth between hope and despair. We had to learn how to turn panic into prayer, prayer into peace, and peace into perseverance.

We all have difficulties from time to time in our life's journeys. How we handle them, how we grow from them, and how we choose to proceed after them are what determines our future.

For us, we feel remarkably blessed that we *have* a future.

Taylor and Gip with Pops (Santa), Uncle Jimmy, Uncle Brian, and cousins Myles and Jonathan.

Taylor and friends at the prom.

Taylor and Gip at Taylor's high school graduation.

Taylor received a football scholarship to Truman State University.

CHAPTER 45

Starting Over

Many have asked us if things are back to normal yet. My honest answer is that we have a *new* normal in our lives now, and we have learned that our acceptance of that is our greatest gift. It's the Serenity Prayer in its purest form: *God grant us the serenity to accept the things we cannot change, the courage to change the things we can, and the wisdom to know the difference.*

When you deal with life-altering situations, you often have to let go of your original life plans and replace them with new ones. That's not easy. Like most parents, Richard and I had hopes and dreams for our children from the moment they were born. It's been our goal to give them a good home, a good education, and a strong root system of Christianity and moral fiber. We had a plan.

But September 6, 2003, was not on our agenda. At that moment, everything in our lives came to a screeching halt. Dreams we once had were immediately replaced with tears and fears. It was heartbreaking to watch it slip away.

We've come a long way, but we are not where we were or who we were before this tragedy. The hardships we've suffered were life-changing. We are not back to normal just because things have settled down. What happened to our family changed us and the course of our lives forever.

But listen closely—I said *changed*, not *destroyed*. Many of the changes have presented amazing opportunities we would not have had without this experience. We've been blessed in ways we never imagined we could be. We've seen angels in this world that perhaps we'd have missed prior to this experience. We've witnessed honor and valor most people never see evidence of. We've been able to reach out to others and share hope, in ways we couldn't have before.

We've had to start over in many ways, but I have no doubt these experiences have changed us in the manner God intended.

CHAPTER 46

Paying It Forward

Being a "receiver" has been a humbling experience. We weren't prepared for the kindness shown to us, and many times we didn't know how to accept it. It was amazing most of the time; our hearts were deeply touched, and we were joyfully overwhelmed. But there were times we felt embarrassed receiving so much attention, and we weren't sure how to process it.

We've done our best to receive gracefully but have learned it's easier said than done. We've also come to realize that you rarely get to give back to those who have given to you. It seems the best way to pay it forward is by listening to the call to help others as so many have answered calls to help us. It's the gift that keeps on giving.

While in the hospital, we were surrounded by other hurting families. In the spirit of "misery loves company," we found great comfort having each other to turn to. But we yearned for more than a listening ear. We wanted tangible evidence of hope for a viable recovery for our loved ones. I would've given anything to have a recovered TBI patient—a Gip Gayle, if you will—walk into our hospital room when we were in the depths of despair.

That's the very reason we go to Shepherd Center to meet with other families. When patients see Gip the way he is now, they often think he couldn't possibly have been as badly injured as they are. We bring our photo album filled with pictures of Gip's journey so they can grasp how broken he was and how far he has come. Hmmm . . . just like my sister Helen's dream told us to do!

Photo album of Gip's journey.

When families look at Gip's miraculous recovery, it helps restore hope for them in their own recoveries. And believe me, hope is a powerful place to rest your weary soul.

When Gip speaks to patients and their families, their eyes light up as he encourages them to keep fighting, to hold on to their faith, and to *never* give up. From a former patient, words like that hold great value.

After being so blessed, our hearts will forever linger in the Shepherd Center hallways. Each time we visit, we reunite with Dr. Leslie and Gip's therapists and nurses. It's quite a hug-fest when Gip walks in, as they revel in the fruits of their labor. They still call him "Miracle Boy," and he grins from ear to ear. We're all thankful that Gip is *able* to give back.

Our family has felt privileged to offer support to other families in desperate need of hope, of help, of God. We know that need only too well. And now we have a "been there, done that" shoulder for other hurting families to lean on. We understand confusion with every breath, fear with every decision, and agony with every defeat. Oh yeah, we've been there!

We've learned a lot through this experience. I can't help but wish we hadn't been so *painfully* educated, but we have to look upon that as a blessing of growth and learn to share it with others. We've found that paying it forward is the best way to move forward.

With Dr. Leslie at one of Gip's Shepherd Center visits with patients.

Gip and Beth visit with Dr. Leslie before meeting with Shepherd Center patients.

Gip visiting his beloved therapists at Shepherd Center.

Gip joining his Shepherd Center "family" before meeting with patients. Front row, from left to right: Ashley Haynes, Jennifer Douglas. Back row, from left to right: Kathy Farris, Brandi Bradford, Margaret Sharp, Gip, and Sean Burage.

CHAPTER 47

God's Story, Not Ours

W hen I started writing this book, it was as if a floodgate opened. I didn't think I had any tears left, but as I've retraced our journey's steps, I found myself reliving the heartaches that came with it. I believe I've shed more tears writing about our experiences than I did while actually living them. Guess I've still got some healing to do.

I've walked away from writing many times, taking much-needed emotional breaks. I felt certain God did not want me to suffer, so I assumed I misunderstood His pressing, and I stopped. Besides, I wondered: who will ever read this? I am a weak vessel. Surely God doesn't want to use little ol' me to spread His word.

After my longest writing break, an eight-month reprieve, I decided to stop completely, even though the lion's share of the work was done. I told myself *and* God that I simply could not finish the task—that it was time to cut my losses and move on, that it just wasn't meant to be. I wrapped up my paperwork, computer disks, and flash drives, and stuck them in a big folder. I carefully laid the folder in my "would've-should've-could've" box in the back of my closet.

In that box I have half-written poems, unfinished song lyrics, and incomplete photo albums. It saddened me to see how many items I had put in that box over the years. I closed the lid and shoved the box onto the top shelf, where I thought it would remain untouched forever—or at least until I put something else in it.

I grabbed my tennis shoes and headed upstairs to hop onto the treadmill, hoping that would release some endorphins (happy juices!) to help me cope with my tough decision.

While on the treadmill, I was overcome with emotion. I'd invested several years of my life, my time, and my tears trying to tell our story. It was sad to think I was laying it all to rest unfinished, all for naught. But the emotions of writing had gotten the best of me, and I didn't think I could finish. I convinced myself I'd made the right decision.

Within thirty minutes, my phone rang. A friend was calling. Her friend's daughter was in critical condition after a tragic car accident. In an effort to bring hope to this hurting mom, my friend had shared Gip's story of survival. They asked if I would come to the hospital.

When I walked into the waiting room, my friend rushed over to hug me. She quickly made introductions, and we all began to talk. Although we had never met, this mom and I had an instant bond. Her daughter was in surgery, and the wait was unbearable. It pained me to see such heartache. I knew how she felt. She began to cry as she said, "Please, tell me about your son."

She asked me about Gip's injuries and what the doctor's first prognosis was. I choked up a bit but answered her questions. She stared at me for a moment. Then she asked, "How did you possibly hold on?"

"It wasn't easy," I said. "I felt completely helpless at times." I paused for a moment and said, "So I wrapped myself in prayer 24/7. It was the only thing I knew to do to find real peace. I had to have faith that God was in charge, so *I* didn't have to be."

I believe that sharing my weaknesses can help others more easily relate to how I found my strength. Like theirs, my world was shattered, and I had to dig deep to deal with it. I am still here, and those in similar situations want to know how I got through it.

I clarified that whatever strength she may have sensed in me was from God. I reminded her that His strength is offered to all who ask for it, and it's unlimited! I then glanced at our mutual friend as I encouraged this mom to be on the lookout for the angels God would send to carry her. I smiled as I shared how they are His hands and feet, explaining that through them she would feel God's presence surround her.

The mom was overwhelmed and unable to speak at first. Then she asked me to pray with her. We prayed for her daughter's healing, and we prayed for peace. She hugged me and thanked me for bringing hope to her breaking heart.

As I was leaving, my friend asked if I had finished writing about our journey. I thanked her for asking but told her that "it just wasn't meant to be."

She pulled me into the ladies' room. With her voice at full pitch, she sternly said, "This is not *your* story to tell, Beth. It's *God's*. And He wants to help others through it. Look what just happened here today."

She leaned in closer and said, "You need to listen to God's calling and finish His work!" She pretty much rendered me speechless. I shivered with emotion as I gave a nod of assent and hugged her goodbye.

I sobbed the whole drive home, asking God for His strength to tell His story. As I walked into my house, I went straight to my closet. I stood there for a while staring at the "would've-should've-could've" box that held my writing folder. I took a deep breath, grabbed it, and with determination like never before I dove back in.

A lot of these pages are tear-stained. But many of them are tears of joy as I have been reminded not only of the heartaches but also of the wondrous blessings. I've tried to communicate our feelings with honesty and transparency. I knew that if I did not bear our weaknesses, I could not show God's strengths. I pray that sharing our struggles and how we overcame them may somehow help others in theirs.

I encourage you not to be defeated by your challenges, but rather to find comfort in believing that God will carry you through them. Do not underestimate His power, for He can conquer insurmountable odds, reaching far beyond anything we could ever think of or hope for. Turn to Him, lean on Him, and trust in Him.

On September 6, 2003, I believe heaven touched earth somehow, as we witnessed a miracle that day. But it's not our miracle; it's God's! And we've been humbled by it ever since.

EPILOGUE

I'm Baaack!

On the five-year anniversary of Gip's accident, Chuck sent out another email. This time he was not *asking* for prayers but rather reflecting upon them. Chuck titled his email "A reflection on God's miracle in Gip's life."

Dear Friends,

I was sitting in church recently when we sang the song "Let It Be Said of Us."

> Let it be said of us
> That the Lord was our passion
> That with gladness we bore
> Every cross we were given
> That we fought the good fight
> That we finished the course
> Knowing within us the power of the risen Lord.
> Let the cross be our glory ~ and the Lord be our song
> By mercy made holy ~ by the Spirit made strong
> Let the cross be our glory ~ and the Lord be our song
> 'Til the likeness of Jesus ~ be through us made known
> Let the cross be our glory ~ and the Lord be our song

As we sang these powerful words, I remembered it was the song we sang at church the morning I found out about Gip's accident. I remember on that day falling to my knees as I was overcome with emotion (at that time we didn't think Gip had a chance to make it). The words to the song were so powerful to me as I reflected on Gip's short but wonderful life. I sent out the first request for people to pray after being awakened in the middle of the night with the news. I was making plans to go see the Gayle family in Savannah later that day.

As we sang the song this time, I realized we had just celebrated Gip's five-year anniversary of the accident. I was overcome again with emotion as I reflected on the words to this song. Gip has definitely fought the good fight with the power of the Lord and sings the praises of the Lord! It is hard to believe it has been five years. I revisited Gip's website this week and was reminded of all the miracles in his life. Gip is doing great! He is living on his own again and attending college at a nearby university. This past summer he served for the second year at Discipleship Focus with Young Life in Pigeon Forge, Tennessee. Gip lives each day as a gift from the

Lord and looks for ways he can serve and help others. Beth often tells me she wants to find ways to thank me for the part I played in Gip's amazing story. The blessings of knowing Gip and being around him and his model of how to live each day are the greatest gift anyone could ever offer me. I, like all of you, am a blessed person for having known Gip and his family. Gip's story reminds me each day to have a positive, thumbs-up attitude in times of difficulty. No matter what I face I know God's presence and power are real, because I have seen it played out in the life of Gip Gayle. Thank you for the part you played in Gip's amazing story and may you continue to believe in the miracles of prayer.

God Bless You,

Chuck

As I share our story with you, we are about to celebrate the nine-year anniversary of Gip's accident—or, as we prefer to call it, the anniversary of God's miracle. In some ways I feel lifetimes away from that fateful day in September 2003. In other ways, it seems like it was just yesterday. We've been on a heartbreaking journey, but God has blessed us many times along the way, and we continue to see His light in Gip's life, in ours.

Today Gip is reclaiming his life. He's loving his return to independence. He's driving again and living on his own. He spends time hanging out with friends, dating, golfing, fishing, and playing tennis and volleyball. He's also involved in several young-adult ministries and outreach programs. In another gift from Chuck Scott and Jeff Foxworthy, Gip has been included in their weekly men's Bible study. And yes, he has returned to his beloved sport of hunting whenever possible.

Thanks to the amazing dedication and support of his college advisor, Shannon Ferketish, Gip has just graduated from Kennesaw State University, where he received a Bachelor of Science degree in Integrative Studies, with a major in leadership and a minor in coaching. Mere words cannot possibly express how our family felt as we watched Gip walk across that stage to accept his college diploma. This is a day we all prayed for—a day many said would never come, yet here we are.

Our child is healthy and happy again. He lives each day with joy in his heart and with determination in every ounce of his body. He remains resolved to conquer whatever challenge he may face and is thankful for the opportunity to give glory to God when he does. He's excited about the career opportunities that lie ahead and looks forward to wherever God is leading him next!

Gip is not just living; he's living life to the fullest, just as God intended!

We've come a long way. As a family, we've all survived and recovered, overcoming obstacles none of us ever expected to face. But with God's amazing grace, we got through it.

Gip and his family rejoice in the magical moment of Gip's graduation from Kennesaw State University. Left to right: Honey, Taylor, Beth, Gip, Richard, and Pops.

Once again, Dr. Donald Leslie (left) and Coach Chuck Scott (right) are at Gip's side, this time to celebrate his miraculous accomplishment of receiving a college degree!

Not only is Gip realizing his dreams, but Taylor is accomplishing his as well. In divine timing that could only be orchestrated by our Heavenly Father, both Taylor and Gip graduated from college in the same week! Taylor graduated from Valdosta State University and Gip from Kennesaw State University. It was a double blessing for our family to celebrate both of our sons at the same time as they reached this long-awaited, hard-earned dream come true.

We are proud to share that Taylor has chosen physical therapy for his career. He has been accepted into Mercer University's Doctor of Physical Therapy program here in Atlanta, Georgia. To make it even more special, he is serving his PT internship at Shepherd Center. How sweet is that?

Our family has bonded a great deal through this experience. We were always a close-knit bunch, but this part of our journey has certainly enriched our relationships with each other—and with God.

Do we still have lessons to learn? Absolutely. Do we still face challenges? Of course we do. But we have a lot to be thankful for. And believe me, *we are!*

Some say we've come full circle since Gip's accident. But that doesn't even begin to describe our journey. Through many ups and downs, praise God . . . with God . . . and through God, our circle is much bigger, our faith much deeper, our understanding much greater.

LEFT: Gip and Taylor proudly celebrate their college graduations together.
RIGHT: Gip at his college graduation with his advisor, Shannon Ferketish.

In the lifetime of an educator, a few students come along that you will never forget. In a personal lifetime, a few people come along that change your life. Gip fits both categories in my life.

—Shannon Ferketish, Kennesaw State University
Director of Integrative Studies Program, Gip's college advisor

The word *amen* means "I believe" or "so be it." It's an expression of hearty assent or conviction. So let me close by saying it loud and clear: "AMEN!" I believe—and I pray you do, too.

They say a picture is worth a thousand words.
Well, here we are today—with heartfelt smiles of heavenly gratitude.
To God be the glory!

Clockwise from left: Beth, Taylor, Gip, and Richard.

Gayle Family Album:
After the Storm

Gip with "family angels" at Honey and Pops's 50th wedding anniversary.

Gip with Aunt Jeanette and Uncle Camille.

Gip and Taylor with Poppi.

Family Christmas photo with Yeller.

Gip with Honey and Pops.

A tender moment with mom.

Annual family "beach muscle contest."
From left to right: Taylor, Jonathan,
Uncle Jimmy, Gip, and Richard.

Gip with
cousins. Left
to right: Myles,
Gip, Jonathan,
Taylor, Nicole,
and Lindsey.

Family beach vacation—
with T-shirts from the
Strides for Strength 5K
race benefit.

Gip and Taylor with their new dog, Sadie.

Gip, Taylor, and friend Jarrett Boston, visiting hospital patients with Jeff Foxworthy.

Gip with Beth's YaYa's.

Gayle family with "Gip's girls" and families.

Gip with Taffy, celebrating LSU's championship team.

Gip with Elaine and Warren Parr, family friends from Louisiana.

Christmas elves, left to right: Uncle Jimmy, Jonathan, Myles, Taylor, and Gip.

Family Christmas photo.

Gip with "Gip's Girls."

Gip and cousin Jonathan parasailing.

A return to fishing.

Gip returns to golfing.

Gip gets back to playing tennis.

Gip and cousin Michael.

Playing volleyball.

Fishing with cousins on Uncle Jimmy's boat.

Navigating the ocean with Uncle Jimmy.

A smile says it all—getting back to life!

Gip with Coach Chuck at his son's football game.

To Gip,
One of the finest men I know!
your friend
Jeff Foxworthy

Gip and Jeff Foxworthy
share their testimonies at
a YL hunting trip held at
Foxworthy's hunting farm.

Back in college, at Kennesaw State University.

Thank you for s
Young Life Ce

Gip, along with Jeff Foxworthy, sharing his story with nearly
8,000 people at a national YL convention in Orlando, Florida.

Gip graduating from Kennesaw State University in
May 2012, with a very proud mom at his side.